Differentiation

RICK WORMELI

FOREWORD BY CAROL ANN TOMLINSON

DifferentiatioN

From Planning to Practice Grades 6–12

Stenhouse Publishers
Portland, Maine

NMSA

National Middle School Association
Westerville, Ohio

Stenhouse Publishers
www.stenhouse.com

National Middle School Association
www.nmsa.org

Credits

Page 82: Adapted from *The Differentiated Classroom*, by Carol Ann Tomlinson. Copyright © 1999. Used by permission of the publisher, Association for Supervision and Curriculum Development.

Page 163: *From How to Differentiate Instruction in Mixed-Ability Classrooms, 2nd Edition*, by Carol Ann Tomlinson. Copyright © 2001. Used by permission of the publisher, Association for Supervision and Curriculum Development.

Library of Congress Cataloging-in-Publication Data

Wormeli, Rick.
   Differentiation : from planning to practice, grades 6–12 / Rick Wormeli; foreword by Carol Ann Tomlinson.
       p. cm.
   Includes bibliographical references and index.
    ISBN 978-1-57110-708-4 (alk. paper)
  1. Individualized instruction. 2. High school teaching. 3. Middle school teaching. I. Title.

LB1031.W67 2007
371.39'4—dc22

                                               2007031730

Cover, interior design, and typesetting by Catherine Hawkes,
Cat & Mouse

Manufactured in the United States of America on acid-free, recycled paper
13 12 11 10   9 8 7 6 5

This book is dedicated to every teacher who chooses to teach all students, not just those easiest to teach, and to all those teachers who take time out of their already very busy schedules to inform policy-makers about sound pedagogy so those policy-makers can make effective decisions regarding instruction and assessment in schools.

Contents

A Final Word: Three Tips to Begin the Journey 139

My first year of teaching was the most puzzling, most compelling, most exciting, most disorienting year I had ever lived—or have yet lived, for that matter. Not only had I not planned to be a teacher, but I had declared loudly and with some frequency that teaching was the last job I wanted on the face of the earth.

That adolescent fervor was born of the year my mother (a lifelong teacher) and I spent in the same building. I was in sixth grade, shy, in a new town, too tall. My daily goal was to go unnoticed—unlikely for a girl who was taller than any boy in the class and who had hair long enough to sit on. In any case, there was no hope for anonymity, because my teachers were my mother's friends and they told her stories that involved me. They weren't tales of horror. Part of my plan to be anonymous was to be so compliant and good that I would never be on a teacher's radar. They were just little snippets from a day, presented to my mom as offerings of friendship by her colleagues who knew that she would be happy to have a verbal snapshot of her only child.

At twelve, I couldn't see the stories as acts of friendship. I felt spied upon, betrayed, and I would *not* become an adult who did that to kids. I would *not*, therefore, be a teacher. My mother was kind enough never to say, "I told you so."

My first year of teaching would have involved steep learning curves under any circumstances, because I had steered clear of an education major and thus had no real knowledge of what teaching was like. At best, I was prepared to "play school"—to mimic what I thought my own teachers had done. And the setting of my first year in the classroom was not a best-case scenario.

I taught in the deep South during the first year of integration in a district so rural that it seemed to have been left off all maps. It seemed as though suspicion and disdain was in the air we breathed, and as though we were all lost in ways more consequential than geographically. Adults in the area earned a livelihood largely by being paid not to farm. Many of the kids I taught had never been on highways. I discovered on the first day I taught that many also did not know the name of the country in which we lived. They were high school students.

Had I landed in a classroom on another planet or in another century, I would not have felt more a foreigner or more displaced in time than when I first entered the lives of my students and a time period that caused me to question my own roots as a human being. That my students had little in the way of the opportunities that I had taken for granted was evident to me early on. What took longer was realizing how many factors in their lives conspired to ensure that they retained that status. School was high on the list of limiting factors.

These were kids, the veteran teachers in the school made clear, who couldn't learn, wouldn't learn, didn't want to learn. They were largely regarded as no-hope kids and were too often taught accordingly.

There were a few teachers in the school, however, who seemed to feel differently about the kids. They saw promise where others saw a vacuum. Their classrooms were energy sources for the kids rather than energy sappers. And the students were different people in the two kinds of classrooms.

I gravitated to the positive teachers at first simply because they seemed to regard me as something more promising than a foreign body that had been thrust into a closed system. Later I stayed close to them because they taught me the most important lessons about teaching that I ever learned.

These were teachers who looked at their work as a calling rather than a job. They not only believed but knew the kids they taught would learn. Most importantly, they never once in my hearing suggested that there was a problem with a student or with a student's family when that student wasn't learning according to design. They simply dug deeper into their personal and professional reservoirs to look for one more way they could explain an idea, draw a student into a discussion, or provide support for success. They were not sanctimonious. They laughed at the quirky (and sometimes simply bizarre) comments of kids—but they never laughed at the kids themselves. I did, however, see them cry with kids on occasion. To this day, those teachers are the teachers I aspire to be.

They taught me many things of value—both practical and philosophical. They taught me to find the teachers who are the learners in a building and to become their friend. They taught me to find the teachers who mean to make the classroom work for each kid and to find the teachers who are less afraid of making mistakes than of standing still.

Had I taught in a school where Rick Wormeli taught, I would have found him, become his friend, and been his student. I feel fortunate to have done the latter two—and sad not to have had the opportunity to share a school setting with him.

Rick's work is not going to move the educator who has a ready supply of "yes, buts" ("I could do this, but there isn't enough time," "I could do this, but the kids aren't responsive," "I could do this, but the room is too small"). Rick's work is for the teacher who wants solutions, who wants to grow.

For those teachers and administrators, Rick offers knowledge that comes from having been in a classroom for a long and rich career and from having studied the best of scholarship about teaching and learning. He anticipates the questions teachers will ask about differentiation and answers them directly and economically. He knows what it feels like to succeed with a student—and what it feels like to fail. He prefers the former and he has developed a boundless repertoire of strategies designed to be catalysts for student success and to diminish the opportunity for students to fail.

Rick knows that good teaching—and high-quality differentiation is really just good teaching—requires proactive planning. He knows that powerful teachers place students in the center stage of plans and see themselves not as lead actors in a play but as directors of student learning.

He knows that powerful teachers proactively plan for the success of every student, both when the teacher is presenting and when the student is making sense of knowledge, ideas, and skills. He knows that curriculum, assessment, and instruction are three interdependent sides of a teaching triangle.

Rick points out that differentiation is a derivative of informed assessment and an imperative for effective instruction of students with "special needs" and goes on to remind us that every student has special needs at some time (or many times) in a school day, a school year, and a school life. Differentiation is what we do if we intend to have every student understand what they are learning, why they are learning it, why they should care, and how it makes them more fully human.

Perhaps the most durable of Rick's contributions to the teacher-learners among us is an affirmation of what psychologist Carol Dweck calls a growth mind-set. The subtext of Rick's work is the statement, "Of course each student can succeed with important ideas and skills. Of course I can figure out how to make that happen. Of course that's my aspiration. Of course I'm willing to do what's necessary to make that happen."

As my first colleagues taught me, that's what it really means to be a teacher.

Carol Ann Tomlinson

Acknowledgments

We are the summation of our lives' experiences, and for me, the most transformational experiences have come in the company of insightful thinkers and doers. I hope I have sufficient brainpower to interpret their wisdom correctly and to advance their ideas compellingly as I weave them with my own.

Whether through their written works, in conversations with me and others, or by their modeling of exemplary teaching and compassionate living, the following individuals have cared enough about students, teachers, and society to share their thinking about teaching, assessment, and differentiated instruction with our profession: Carolyn Coil, Robert Marzano, David Sousa, Marilee Sprenger, Jim Grant, Char Forsten, Betty Hollas, Debbie Silver, Amy Benjamin, Sheryn Northey, Carolyn Chapman, Pat Wolfe, Robert Sylwester, Carol O'Connor, Diane Heacox, Tom Guskey, Ken O'Connor, Susan Brookhart, Susan Winebrenner, Kylene Beers, Linda Rief, William Bender, Deborah Blaz, Kay Burke, Gayle Gregory, Sandra Kaplan, Cindy Strickland, Rita King, Judy Dodge, Mel Levine, Rick Lavoie, Robin Fogarty, Gretchen Goodman, Donna Whyte, Gloria Fender, Kelly Gallagher, Alfred Tatum, Stephanie Harvey, Carol Glynn, Stephen McCarney, Jay McTighe, Grant Wiggins, Ruby Payne, William Purkey, Joseph Renzulli, Jerome Bruner, Spence Rogers, Paula Rutherford, Richard Strong, Harvey Silver, Matthew Perini, Linda Tilton, Cris Tovani, Thomas Armstrong, Bruce Campbell, Eric Jensen, Roger Taylor, Robert Sternberg, Barbara Strauch, Marcia Tate, Susan Nolen, Catherine Taylor, and Rick Stiggins. In addition, I am indebted to the faculties of Langley High School, Oakton High School, Freedom Hill Elementary School, Herndon Middle School, and Rachel Carson Middle School, all of which are in Fairfax

County Public Schools in northern Virginia, one of the best districts in the world to learn the craft of teaching diverse populations. I am in their debt.

One contributor to the differentiated instruction world deserves special mention: Carol Ann Tomlinson. There are many voices out there talking about differentiation, but Carol is the pioneer who put differentiation on the map for most of us. She has not only showed us how vital differentiation is to our schools' success, particularly as we teach the masses in a democratic society, but she also explains how to do it in practical yet eloquent terms. Her work is the catalyst for literally thousands of educators' thinking around the globe. I can't wait to see what she comes up with next. And besides all that, she's a former middle school teacher, and that's cool.

Readers have seen the names of Stenhouse Publishers' staff members often in an author's acknowledgments, and that's because they are talented and helpful people. They deserve every accolade. I am very thankful for the advice of Philippa Stratton, Bill Varner, and Erin Trainer, and, in particular, Holly Holland, an author and the first editor of my columns for *Middle Ground* magazine as well as the editor of my first book, *Meet Me in the Middle*. She's the one who put the idea in my head that I might have something to share, and it has changed my life. Thank you, Holly.

I am also grateful to Brenda Dyck, Chris Toy, Bill Ivey, John Norton, Cossondra George, Marsha Ratzel, Ellen Berg, and many others on the MiddleTalk email list and everyone on the Teacher Leader's Network email list for setting high standards of thinking, compassion, and professionalism.

As always, I am most grateful to my family. My wife, Kelly, is both Mom and Dad when I travel to work with schools. While holding a full-time position in her company, she manages our household, including coordinating and driving our two children to multiple sports and music commitments. She's an amazing person. My son, Ryan, and my daughter, Lynn, are both in high school now. With each passing year, I grow more and more excited to see the wonderful young adults they are becoming. Somehow Kelly and I have added two more thoughtful citizens to the planet who will one day become terrific parents for the next generation. I thank both Ryan and Lynn for every bout of laughter, every conversation about life, and every candid question about adults' hypocrisy they ask. By answering their questions honestly, I confront my own complacency and, paraphrasing Charles DuBois, sacrifice what I am for what I could become.

Rick Wormeli
Herndon, VA
2007

Chapter 1

Developing a Common Frame of Reference

Rationale

You already know how to differentiate a lesson. You've been employing a variety of developmentally responsive strategies throughout the school year. Here are some examples from your current practices:

After your lesson about Renaissance art, a student calls you over to her desk, tells you she's confused, and asks you to explain the main points again. You do so, providing extra examples that she can reference while she completes the chapter summary you previously assigned. With the new information, she's able to work independently.

A student is struggling to draw a perfect circle for part of another project. You just happen to be carrying a roll of masking tape in your hand, which you now tap against the student's desk, pondering aloud, "Hmm. I wonder what you could use as a tracing guide to create a circle.... There has to be something here that you can use." The student grins, grabs the tape, turns it flat against his paper, and traces the inside contour of the roll. "Thanks," he says as he hands the roll back to you.

A student has a learning disability in reading. You record one of the history textbook's chapters on a compact disc or audiocassette so he can listen to your clarifying vocal inflections while he reads the text silently. This practice increases his comprehension of Winston Churchill's life, which enables him to fully participate in class discussions about the world leader.

A student finds wide-ruled paper too cumbersome to use. She stretches her letters to fill the lines and, consequently, her handwriting sprawls illegibly. You suggest that she use college-ruled paper, which has narrower spaces between the lines. She makes the switch, and her handwriting improves.

A student has intense test anxiety, particularly with written exams. While testing students' knowledge of safety rules in your Technology and Innovations course, you call the worried student over to a quiet area at the back of the classroom and ask the test questions orally. Occasionally, you let the student draw something on paper to demonstrate his understanding. He takes the test this way, and you get an accurate assessment of his skills.

In science class, a student is struggling to identify a leaf while using a reference book. She easily classifies her specimen as a leaf and not a clump of needles, then moves to the section of the book discussing deciduous trees. Here the book asks her to consider whether the leaf's veins are parallel or pinnate (some vein patterns run parallel, but those that branch out are called *pinnate*). The student doesn't fully understand the difference, so she skips that part of the book and quickly turns the pages, searching for a drawing that looks similar to her specimen. After a few minutes, she selects an illustration. It's not an exact match, but she records the name under her drawing of her leaf in her lab notebook and moves to the next specimen. You stop her and ask her to reexamine the veins in the drawing and compare them with the veins of her specimen.

"Are they the same?" you ask.

"No," she replies.

"Then you have not found the correct name for the leaf. How do the veins run in your specimen?" you ask, tracing the parallel veins of the leaf with your finger.

"I don't know, straight?" she says.

You nod. "Correct. They are not crooked, and they're not perpendicular. They're ..." you lead her.

"Parallel?"

You nod again. "So this is parallel. What's the other type of veinage called?"

The student scans through her leaf terminology list. "Pinnate?"

"Yes. What does it look like?"

"Like little *v*'s or branches," she says.

"Good. Remember the pinnate veinage for later specimens. But for this one, focus only on leaves with parallel veinage. Each characteristic helps you narrow the focus to the final, correct leaf."

You make a mental note to give this student more time to investigate taxonomies. *Maybe some extra practice categorizing objects would be helpful for her*, you think, then record the observation on a pad of sticky notes you carry in your pocket for observations like this. You walk over and place the note with the information on it into your lesson-plan book so you'll see it later as you prepare for tomorrow's class.

Sound strategies, flexible methods, and good results. The genie disappears into his lamp when you realize that you won't need his assistance after all: There's nothing magical or overly complex about differentiated instruction.

It's that easy. We're finished explaining here.

Well, not entirely. There might be a few more ideas to add to your "bag of tricks," but differentiation really is that straightforward. When we differentiate, we do whatever it takes to help students learn by providing individual accommodations and making adjustments to our general lesson plans. There are no hidden secrets saved only for the most honored of practitioners. Adjusting lessons, homework assignments, classroom procedures, and assessments to meet students where they are—struggling, advanced, or in between—and making sure they've mastered their subjects is simply good teaching. And it is both possible and powerful for every educator.

Differentiation is one of the most popular terms found in school improvement plans these days. It's a very effective focus for schools but some educators claim to be providing differentiated instruction, assessment, and curriculum when reality reveals otherwise. Many educators write long, complicated professional development plans, summarizing how they will learn to differentiate over the next few years. These expressed intentions often get stuffed into classroom bookshelves and are never reopened because of teachers' over-extended schedules and administrators' shifting priorities. Other educators think differentiation is a passing fad and don't bother to interrupt their normal classroom routines to provide it.

I invite readers to look at differentiation through a more accurate and historical lens. If you read descriptions of teaching in ancient Greece and Egypt, for example, you'll find repeated evidence of differentiation. It's among the most traditional forms of instruction. In fact, *not* differentiating is the short-lived fad. A one-size-fits-all education won't work any longer, if it ever did. Consider the following:

- Students are more diverse than ever—culturally, emotionally, economically, physically, and intellectually.

- The public wants educators to be held accountable for students' success, no matter their circumstances.

- Our students must be prepared to compete in the global economy, which requires an increasing level of knowledge and skills.

- Mental dexterity is the new currency. A country's most important exports include its citizens' ability to innovate and solve problems. Today's students must learn how to continually manage, critique, and increase their knowledge. To cultivate these capacities in all students, including those who are ready to move beyond the regular education standards, we will need to expand and adapt our own practices as well.

- We have accumulated a critical mass of new and compelling research about how the human brain learns and can use this information to transform our instruction and assessment methods. Ignoring these data is a form of educational malpractice. Meeting the needs of diverse learners isn't whimsical. It's imperative.

Effective differentiation is what most of us have been striving to accomplish since our first days in the classroom. The direct, observable results of differentiation provide the meaningful experiences that motivate us to show up every day.

Yet, in spite of the greater resources and research at our disposal, many teachers still struggle with the practicalities of adjusting their lessons for students who struggle, learn differently, or need more challenge. When we try to differentiate for 150 to 250 students a day over five or six class periods, the task can seem staggering. We feel like we are drowning in a sea of pressure from increasing numbers of stakeholders, new school district directives, and overwhelming student loads. It's no wonder we choose not to extend ourselves completely every day; otherwise our energy would be depleted early in the school year. During these times, we may use teaching practices just because they're habitual or easy. We don't really know whether these strategies work, particularly with diverse students.

I've had this mind-set from time to time in my own career. As uncomfortable as it is to admit this, sometimes I retreated into survival mode and just focused on getting through the day. I console myself with the thought that this retrenchment only occurred occasionally. I recommend that you give yourself similar dispensation for these incidental lapses.

After thoroughly exploring differentiated approaches, however, I am rejuvenated, and I think you will be as well. Differentiated instruction provides both principles and techniques for excellent teaching. It's an effective sword against complacency. We can raise the bar, aiming for sound pedagogy—differentiation—at least 90 percent of the time. We may not be able to eliminate all the pressures, but we can search for ways to teach smarter, not harder. And through our searching, we find meaning and the energy to continue. This book provides an informed response to that quest.

Differentiated Instruction in the Classroom

Let's examine some applications of differentiated instruction to see the concept in context. Read the following description of a math lesson. Identify where the teacher uses differentiation to meet her students' needs.

* * *

Jane Greateducator is introducing a unit about adding and subtracting integers. She first draws a thermometer vertically on the chalkboard and labels the degree markings from −20 to +20. She places arrows at either end of the line to indicate that the numbers would continue in each direction. She gives several students who learn more when working with manipulatives actual thermometers, borrowed from the science classroom.

On the drawn thermometer, she places a dot on the mark for +15 degrees and then says to the class, "If the temperature was plus 15, and it dropped eighteen degrees during the night, what temperature would it be?" She asks the students with the real thermometers to place their fingernails at the identified points along the thermometer, reminding them that they may need to rotate the instrument along its horizontal axis in order to read the markings.

Most of the students follow the markings with their eyes until they reach the eighteenth one. Some students sit and wait for others to complete the task. One student raises his hand, and the teacher calls his name. The student says, "Negative 3 degrees?"

"Correct," says Ms. Greateducator. "Now show us how you figured it out."

She hands the student a piece of chalk. He takes the chalk and walks to the board, placing the chalk's point at the +15 degree mark on the drawn thermometer. He moves the chalk down the thermometer, counting off the degree marks as he goes. When he gets to the eighteenth mark down, he stops and circles it.

"Nicely done," Ms. Greateducator says, adding, "And what if the temperature was minus 7 degrees and it rose ten degrees? What would the new temperature be?"

The student puts the point of the chalk at the −7 degree mark, then counts the marks as he moves up the thermometer. The student circles the new temperature reading and declares, "Plus 3 degrees."

"Correct again," says Ms. Greateducator. "Thank you. You may take your seat." She then asks the class to figure out the new temperature readings and fill in the chart that she previously provided to them.

Original Temperature	Adjustment	New Temperature
+15	Drops 20 degrees	
−17	Rises 6 degrees	
−20	Rises 21 degrees	
+10	Drops 9 degrees	

Ms. Greateducator provides time for students to determine the new temperatures accurately. Some students ask their peers with the real thermometers if they can borrow the instruments. As students work independently, the teacher moves around the room and asks clarifying questions, occasionally providing supportive comments when students correctly identify the new temperatures.

Next, Ms. Greateducator asks her students to create mathematical equations using the data from the chart. She notices that one student has already raced ahead, completing the assignment correctly with all four scenarios from the chart. She smiles at him and continues explaining the principles to the rest of the class, using the first two sample scenarios as models.

"The temperature was plus 15 degrees and it dropped eighteen degrees, so the new temperature is negative 3 degrees." As she says this, she writes, $+15 - 18 = -3$.

She continues: "The temperature was negative 7 degrees, and it rose ten degrees, so the new temperature is plus 3 degrees." As she says this, she writes, $-7 + 10 = +3$.

Now she asks students to follow her example and write the equations for the four samples in the chart. She gives them two minutes to finish the assignment. The student who completed the task on his own is no longer paying attention, and Ms. Greateducator frowns at him. He ignores her and continues molding two paper clips into a tension-release, launching mechanism that leaps three feet into the air.

* * *

Now, let's step back and examine Ms. Greateducator's lesson. A quick look would establish several points of differentiation:

- The teacher knows that some of her students are still at a concrete level of thinking. They have to touch things to make sense of them. They are not yet comfortable with abstract reasoning. So, she places real thermometers in their hands in addition to the symbolic representation drawn on the chalkboard.

- She also moves from the concrete task of following marks on a thermometer to the symbolic portrayal of the mathematical concept through the equations and the vertical number line.

- She prevents potential stumbling blocks by advising students to hold the thermometers so they can read the markings clearly.

- The teacher knows that just telling students how to add and subtract integers will not ensure that they learn the mathematical concepts. They need to visualize the process. Her "hook" for this is the thermometer. Later in the lesson, she'll turn the thermometer sideways to introduce an integer number line (negative numbers on the left, positive numbers on the right), and repeat the practice tasks of starting with one number and moving a specific number of points in a negative or positive direction.

- She moves around the room and answers individual questions, guiding students as they practice.

- She provides structure in the form of the chart for students to complete.

- She gives students ample time to absorb new information.

- She asks the volunteer student to explain his thinking so the class has a model to use or adapt.

However, just like all of us, Ms. Greateducator missed some opportunities to differentiate. Here are some additional ways she might have approached the lesson.

- She could have preassessed students to find out what they already knew about integers. If she had, she would have noticed that at least one student already had mastered the essential skills and needed more complex assignments to extend his knowledge.

- When she did find out that one student already knew how to manipulate integers, Ms. Greateducator just smiled at him but did nothing to engage him beyond the initial activity. She hadn't prepared enrichment activities for students who learn quickly.

- Some students sat at their desks and didn't complete the tasks. Ms. Greateducator could have anticipated this by developing an alternate activity or using constructive strategy to reengage them.

As you read this scene, you probably noticed that much of this analysis referred to effective teaching techniques, not esoteric or specialized instruction. That's the point. Although we may plan the majority of the lesson, we also can use differentiation informally, whenever the need arises. We could look at any description of any lesson by any teacher and find several examples of differentiation as well as several missed opportunities. Experience will increase our options and resolve, but there will always be room for improvement. Being flexible and attentive is vital to differentiation.

Defining Differentiated Instruction

Differentiation is foremost a professional and responsive mind-set. The following reflective questions seem to establish that mind-set most effectively:

- Are we willing to teach in whatever way is necessary for students to learn best, even if the approach doesn't match our own preferences?

- Do we have the courage to do what works, not just what's easiest?

- Do we actively seek to understand our students' knowledge, skills, and talents so we can provide an appropriate match for their learning needs? And once we discover their individual strengths and weaknesses, do we actually adapt our instruction to respond to their needs?

- Do we continually build a large and diverse repertoire of instructional strategies so we have more than one way to teach?

- Do we organize our classrooms for students' learning or for our teaching?

- Do we keep up-to-date on the latest research about learning, students' developmental growth, and our content specialty areas?

- Do we ceaselessly self-analyze and reflect on our lessons—including our assessments—searching for ways to improve?

- Are we open to critique?

- Do we push students to become their own education advocates and give them the tools to do so?

Dr. John Lounsbury (2006), a pioneer of the middle school movement, reminds us that some classrooms are designed to meet the teacher's needs more than the students' needs.

One example of this would be the location of the teacher's desk. If it's front and center in the classroom, based on the premise that the teacher can keep an eye on all students from a central location, the impact may be twofold: (1) students will get the unspoken yet clear message that the teacher and his or her work are more important than their own, and (2) the teacher will be less inclined to leave his or her command post and move to students' work spaces. Instead, with a quick wave of the teacher's hand, students are told to come to the teacher's desk for assistance.

Another example is when teachers use themselves as the pivot point for class discussions; each response from a student must bounce back to the teacher before anyone else can comment. Whoever responds to students is doing the majority of the learning, so teachers should get out of the way and encourage students to naturally and routinely respond directly to their classmates. Teachers who keep the discussion revolving around their own ideas are well-intentioned but misinformed gatekeepers who need to change their tactics from declarations of truth to questions that guide thinking, and that's only if what is stated by students is somehow false.

Lounsbury's caution is well taken: Do we organize our lessons around students' learning the curriculum or around our dissemination of it? In other words, is our focus on what students are learning or on what we're teaching? Successful teachers think and speak in terms of what students are learning, not what they are presenting.

- Do we regularly close the gap between knowing what to do and actually doing it?

Many teachers and schools have the knowledge and tools to accommodate English language learners (ELLs), improve the performance of underachieving students, provide appropriate challenges for advanced learners, and motivate reluctant learners, but they choose not to address all of their needs. The reasons for their inadequate responses include complacency, cynicism, fear, distrust, unclear outcomes, real or perceived increases in their workload, and the belief that their hands are tied and they can't fight the system. Teachers who are committed to excellence for all actively seek to close the gap between knowing and doing. They find ways to renew themselves, beat an ineffective system, build trust, and stay healthy; they rarely coast. More importantly, they try something else if what they are currently doing isn't working for students. They are motivated by sentiments similar to those expressed by paraplegic and rock band manager James Neil Hollingworth, AKA Ambrose Redmoon: "Courage is the not the absence of fear, but rather the judgement that something else is more important than that fear." In their mind-set, then, these teachers regularly ask themselves what they consider so important that it eclipses their fears, and they take physical and mental steps to pursue those actions.

The two simple charges of differentiation are: (1) do whatever it takes to maximize students' learning instead of relying on a one-size-fits-all, whole-class method of instruction and (2) prepare students to handle anything in their current and future lives that is not differentiated, i.e., to become their own learning advocates.

We often describe differentiation with the phrase, "doing what's fair" for students, which refers to the process of designing developmentally appropriate instruction and assessments. When we differentiate, we finesse the learning for students while finessing students for their learning. We don't just adapt our instructional techniques to meet their needs; we prepare students for the variety of learning and life situations they will encounter. So, while we may show students that they have a proclivity for visual-spatial thinking and suggest that they might want to record the lecture notes as a series of drawings and visual metaphors, we also teach them how to get better at expressing their thinking through the written word. This dexterity—adjusting both curriculum and students' skills to make sure students learn successfully—is critical during students' formal schooling.

In the world beyond school, we gravitate toward work and hobbies in which we excel; we self-differentiate. As a result, we don't need as many differentiated support systems as we did in school. We graduate with a specific skill set that matches an employer's needs. We agree to perform jobs that don't require a steep learning curve, and we don't have to be good at everything at once. If something comes up in the job that we don't know how to do, we draw upon our life experience and adult-level competencies. We can learn new skills, break tasks into smaller steps and formats we can handle, work collaboratively with colleagues who have skills that complement our own, or harness the resources and training necessary to do our jobs well. If these actions don't help us succeed, we may seek other employment.

In schools, however, we require students to learn and be good at everything, regardless of their proclivities, readiness levels, cultural barriers, learning deficiencies, or learning styles. We insist that students know how to analyze poetry, paint a picture that reflects a particular style of art, write essays, solve calculus problems, balance chemical equations, debate civic issues, remember historical events, defend their opinions about sovereign governments, use multiple computer software programs, acquire vocabulary, keep up proper hygiene, speak publicly, maintain friendships, navigate adolescence, demonstrate positive morality, ask probing questions, remember multiple tasks, organize their school supplies, and turn in their work on time—and this is just on Monday.

Keep in mind that no two students are the same. Some excel in certain fields, some in others, and some seem to learn quickly or not at all. Unfortunately, our schools are set up to push them through the education paces at a single speed. Everyone at a specific grade level is expected to learn a particular set of skills, and everyone at another grade level is expected to learn another set. There is an assumption that we are working with the same raw resources, all in the same condition, all with the same needs, and all growing at the same rate. This thinking goes against everything we know about messy, organic human learning. To mitigate the harmful effects of this approach, we differentiate, giving every student a fighting chance to be not just competent but excellent, while finding meaning in learning as well.

Let me be clear: Differentiation is not about requiring less or more work from students of varying degrees of readiness. We don't ask advanced students to do two book reports while struggling students do one. Instead, we change the nature of the work, not its quantity. Differentiation means we increase what students can achieve, and that takes focused work on everyone's part.

It's in the *un*differentiated classes that students can coast along, rarely challenged, rationalizing that teachers don't care or that struggling in school implies stupidity. In the undifferentiated classes, teachers present material, then test and document students' deficiencies. In the differentiated classes, however, teachers take the time to know their students. And, armed with that information, they make learning so compelling that students have no choice but to become engaged. These teachers are keenly aware of how students need to grow, and they make adjustments to ensure that those gains occur.

This approach takes courage. For example, a student may understand a concept very well but not yet be a proficient writer. Do we make her demonstrate her understanding through the essay that we've assigned to the rest of the class? If so, that would test her ability to write an essay, not measure what she knows about the topic at hand. Will we follow our professional instincts and test this student differently than her classmates? Do we believe that we can hold her accountable for the same universal factors that we expect her classmates to learn, no matter the assessment format? And can we explain this approach clearly to other students, parents, colleagues, and administrators who question the fairness of it? If we want an accurate portrayal of a student's mastery of a particular concept, the assessment format we use must enable us to determine that. This is differentiation.

Consider another scenario: A student still doesn't understand what we're teaching even after what we consider to be a very thorough lesson. Do we blame the student, or do we reexamine what we could do to clarify the concepts for the child? Do we reteach, provide more examples, extend the time in which he can learn, incorporate different technology, analyze the student's specific challenges, approach the lesson from a different angle, provide a quick reference tool when studying sophisticated concepts, use a better metaphor, or do something else? If we teach so that students learn, we do whatever it takes to make this happen. This is differentiation.

For a gifted student, do we assume she'll understand the lesson just because she's been identified as academically advanced? Do we assume she'll find something of value from our lessons aimed at the middle performers because she knows how to learn on her own? If so, then why do we make gifted students come to school—for socialization? Not good enough. They don't all learn on their own. Gifted students need instruction that is dynamic, brave, and focused on their needs, just as struggling students do. This is differentiation.

What about a student who doesn't understand the lesson by the time you've finished teaching it? Given a few more days or even a couple of weeks, he probably will. Some teachers might tell this student, "It's too bad you didn't learn it on that first Wednesday in November, the day of the test. Now, a week later, you can go back and try to learn it because it's important to your education, but I won't give you full credit." Would you agree with this approach? I hope not. It does *not* reflect differentiation.

This is the major component of differentiation: the mind-set. Everything else is craft. We can't get to the craft—the tips for management and orchestration of the differentiated lesson—unless our mind grasps this liberating emphasis. The lesson-plan ideas that follow will become very comfortable once you embrace the differentiation mind-set. If you are struggling with this principle, you may find it challenging to proceed, but go ahead and give the lesson a try. The mind-set will come as you work with your students and experience their success. While reading the ideas I have presented, ask yourself the questions listed on pages 8–9. Consider whether these ideas validate what you already know and, if they do, whether or not you act upon these beliefs in the classroom. If these ideas are new to you, consider going along with the thinking until your experience catches up. Our students are counting on your resoundingly affirmative response.

How to Extend These Processes to Any Subject

There is no single, tried-and-true method of differentiating instruction and assessment for all students. We do whatever works. However, there are some commonly accepted practices that can help teachers design more effective and responsive lessons. These practices are presented in the pages ahead.

As you read, you may find that the subject matter or the grade levels represented differ from yours. Please don't dismiss these examples as irrelevant to your work. The ideas still apply to you, the teacher who is learning to differentiate or the teacher who is refining his or her practices. Read the examples for the procedures, not the specific content of the lessons. If the examples happen to incorporate strategies you can actually use in your classroom, that's wonderful! Feel free to adapt and improve them. If the examples fall outside your domain, pull out the general practices you find helpful as you design lessons pertinent to your teaching situation. The practices presented here are universally applicable, whether you teach fifth grade or twelfth grade, language arts, or calculus.

For example, at some point in the process of designing our lessons, we all have to identify what we'll accept as evidence of students' mastery of the topic. Do students have to memorize the information and pull it out of their heads with no help from us, or will they be allowed to choose the correct answer from a list, such as on a multiple-choice exam? Will they be allowed to demonstrate proficiency orally? How about artistically? Only in writing? Whether we're teaching sixth graders how to solve for a variable, eighth graders about due process in a civics class, or eleventh graders the formulas for determining force and motion in physics, we still have to determine what is most important for them to know and how they can show us that they know it. So, whatever your specialty, there's information here that you can use. Read for the universal procedures, practice with your particular lessons.

In the margins of several of the examples, you will find captions that point out practical and procedural tips. I included these to remind you about key ideas that you will want to carry forward and apply to your own lessons. We left the margins wide in this book so you could have space to mark text and write your thinking next to it.

The lessons and the responses to "What if?" scenarios are by no means comprehensive. They couldn't be, given the variety of our students, the breadth of our curricula, and the potential of our imaginations. Consider them launching points for your own ideas; use them, add to them, or revise them any way you'd like. And be sure at some point to share your new strategies with colleagues. We're all waiting for your insights.

So begin to explore the ideas, close the gap between knowing and doing, and improve the learning experiences of tomorrow's amazing leaders—our students.

Chapter 2

A Walk-Through of a Differentiated Lesson

Overview

Finally, a moment to sit down and plan next week's lessons. Your students are returning home by this point in the afternoon. You drop off some papers in the front office, head back to your classroom, and sit down at your desk. You notice some professional development handouts from presentations on differentiated instruction stacked neatly in the corner.

In front of you is a blank sheet of paper or a computer screen ready to be filled with your first differentiated lesson, in keeping with your school or school district mandates. Any moment now, your muse will strike. Let the brilliant differentiation begin!

Wait a minute, you think. *When was the last time I watered those plants on the windowsill? And didn't I want to rearrange the seating chart today?* Well, you reason, *the differentiated lesson plan can wait a few more moments while I attend to other important matters.*

And still the cursor pulses expectantly upon the computer screen ... waiting.

Okay, okay, you say to yourself. *Stop procrastinating. It can't be that bad. It might seem overwhelming at first, but I'm a professional educator—I can do this.*

And, indeed, you can. You won't believe how natural and meaningful differentiation will become once you've completed a few lessons. There will come a point, too, when you wonder why you ever worried about differentiation.

Let's begin for real. The following sample lesson will be divided into three parts:

1. Steps to take *before* designing the learning experiences

2. Steps to take *while* designing and implementing the learning experiences

3. Steps to take *after* providing the learning experiences

For clarity's sake, we'll refer to anything you do with students to teach them the material and skills reflected in your lesson plans as "learning experiences." This term encompasses anything and everything we might provide our students in the course of learning.

Each of these three parts will include subparts, but this is the basic sequence that you will follow when planning each lesson. Begin to think this way: What do I do *before* and *while designing* the learning experiences, and what do I think about *after providing* those experiences?

Here is a quick summary of each part with its components. I will explain these in more detail later in this chapter.

Steps to Take Before *Designing the Learning Experiences*

1. Identify your essential understandings, questions, benchmarks, objectives, skills, standards, and/or learner outcomes.

2. Identify those students who have special needs, and start thinking about how you will adapt your instruction to ensure they can learn and achieve.

3. Design formative and summative assessments.

4. Design and deliver preassessments based on summative assessments and identified objectives.

5. Adjust assessments and objectives based on further thinking while designing assessments.

Steps to Take While *Designing and Implementing the Learning Experiences*

1. Design the learning experiences for students based on the information gathered from those preassessments; your knowledge of your students; and your expertise with the curriculum, cognitive theory, and students at this stage of human development.

2. Run a mental tape of each step in the lesson sequence to make sure that the process makes sense for your diverse group of students and will help the lesson run smoothly.

3. Review your plans with a colleague.

4. Obtain/create materials needed for the lesson.

5. Conduct the lesson.

6. Adjust formative and summative assessments and objectives as necessary based on observations and data collected while teaching the lessons.

Steps to Take After *Providing the Learning Experiences*

1. With students, evaluate the lesson's success. What evidence do you have that students grasped the important concepts and skills? What worked and what didn't, and why?

2. Record advice about possible changes to make when you repeat this lesson in future years.

Figure 2.1 lists these steps in a chart form, and they are also in the Appendix for easy reference.

The majority of the text in the lesson that follows reflects the behind-the-scenes thinking that goes on as you design your differentiated lesson. The specific steps involved in that designing, however, are listed again at the end. Although your pedagogy and priorities may differ from mine in certain places, I can assure you that the sequence has proven effective in class after class, week after week, and year after year. Feel free to deviate from the format as necessary to meet the unique needs of the students you serve, but keep the basics, if possible.

Remember: While this lesson focuses on world history and early explorers, in particular, the same universal principles of differentiated lesson design apply whether we are teaching advanced literary analysis, complex scientific processes, or irrational numbers. It's worth the time no matter what you teach to visit the thinking behind each step. In Chapter 5, we'll explore specific differentiated approaches for a variety of curricular areas.

Steps to Take *Before* Designing the Learning Experiences

Identify Your Essential Understandings, Questions, Benchmarks, Objectives, Skills, Standards, and/or Learner Outcomes

How long should it take for a teacher to determine the objectives for a differentiated lesson or unit? Twenty minutes? An hour? For first-timers, creating an effective differentiated unit or lesson might take one or two

FIGURE 2.1 Three Stages of Planning for Differentiated Lessons

Steps to Take *Before* Designing the Learning Experiences	Steps to Take *While* Designing and Implementing the Learning Experiences	Steps to Take *After* Providing the Learning Experiences
1. Identify your essential understandings, questions, benchmarks, objectives, skills, standards, and/or learner outcomes. 2. Identify those students who have special needs, and start thinking about how you will adapt your instruction to ensure they can learn and achieve. 3. Design formative and summative assessments. 4. Design and deliver preassessments based on summative assessments and identified objectives. 5. Adjust assessments and objectives based on further thinking while designing assessments.	1. Design the learning experiences for students based on the information gathered from those preassessments; your knowledge of your students; and your expertise with the curriculum; cognitive theory; and students at this stage of human development. 2. Run a mental tape of each step in the lesson sequence to make sure that the process makes sense for your diverse group of students and will help the lesson run smoothly. 3. Review your plans with a colleague. 4. Obtain/create materials needed for the lesson. 5. Conduct the lesson. 6. Adjust formative and summative assessments and objectives as necessary based on observation and data collected while teaching the lessons.	1. With students, evaluate the lesson's success. What evidence do you have that students grasped the important concepts and skills? What worked and what didn't, and why? 2. Record advice about possible changes to make when you repeat this lesson in future years.

Give yourself time to figure out what's important to teach.

weeks. This extended time period may be necessary to (a) understand the content yourself and (b) make sure you are teaching what the school, governing body, and experts in your discipline expect. Few things are as frustrating as spending six weeks on a topic and discovering that there is only one short question about it on the state or provincial exam. In addition, experts in our field might cringe at our misinterpretations or misrepresentations of particular topics. Our students and our communities are depending on us to teach the material accurately and comprehensively.

Figuring out what is accurate and important to teach students is a critical step in our lesson design. Most teachers recognize that there are too many standards and objectives in the modern curriculum to address in daily fifty-minute periods over the course of a single school year. Although we may follow district-mandated pacing guides, we won't be able to do justice to everything listed in most disciplines.

On top of that, we often disagree with one another. Curriculum is very relative and subjective. For example, who decides that direct and indirect objects must be taught to eleven- and twelve-year-olds? Is it appropriate for all students, regardless of musical interest, to learn the difference between the treble and bass clefs? Should everyone memorize Abraham Lincoln's "Gettysburg Address"? Why or why not? What does every functioning citizen really need to know about sine and cosine, and why do they need to know these mathematical functions?

Compare your thinking with colleagues when identifying what to teach.

As someone who is deeply interested in the varied ecosystems within the world's oceans, I can't believe anyone could teach ocean ecology without incorporating the correct terms for the stratified marine biome: benthic, pelagic, and euphotic. Yet many schools teach marine systems without mentioning these basic designations and, much to my frustration and our civilization's great peril, some educators focus on oceans only as one of several biomes to memorize for a geography quiz. Of course, just as I am fighting for what I consider essential in a given discipline, other teachers are championing their causes. It may be difficult to find time to get together with colleagues and discuss our differences, but it's important that we do. It's too easy to get myopic and territorial.

In a differentiated classroom, we have an additional factor to consider: Must *all* students learn the same skills and concepts? Given what we know about our students, is a particular standard or outcome developmentally appropriate for them? For example, some students may not be ready to receive what we have to offer them. Do we try to cram the concepts into their craniums anyway?

Are the grade-level standards appropriate for every student?

No. This doesn't do anyone any good. There will be situations in which some students are ready to soar past the identified objectives while their classmates are stumbling over those same goals. If a student has an individualized education plan, we consult the caseworker or special education coordinator to see if the established standards for the subject and grade level are appropriate. If they are, then we adjust the process by which the student learns the information, the product used to demonstrate mastery, or the classroom environment that will enable and stimulate growth.

If the student is not identified as needing special education services yet still struggles to meet the standards, we take a step back and evaluate: Should we change the way the curriculum is clustered or connected? How about an alternative pathway to the same standard of performance? Maybe we need to change the student's seat or writing instrument or suggest a different product to express his knowledge. Perhaps his lackluster performance is rooted in emotional problems rather than developmental delays; we might need to consult the student's counselor or the school social worker or psychologist. If a student hasn't been successful with the initial approach, we search for another way.

The greater gift to students and to the school's mission is to do what's developmentally appropriate for students, which means being a bit pushy about what works for students at each point in their learning. We want students moving along a continuum from early concept attainment to full mastery instead of a lockstep, unresponsive curriculum march toward final exams.

We also must consider whether it is important for all students, including those who are struggling, to learn at the same pace. Or, is it more important that each student learns the material, regardless of whether his or her understanding develops at this particular moment in the grading period? Should those students who can't keep up suffer the consequences?

Adjust the curriculum so students can learn.

Our duty is to teach so that students learn. If it takes a student longer to learn something that her classmates grasped earlier, who cares? It goes against everything we've ever learned about how humans grow and develop to require all students to reach the same level of mastery as everyone else on one particular day during the fourth week of January. It doesn't matter when during the grading period that a student learns something; what matters is that she eventually does. If we teach or grade in a way that causes a student to lose hope, we've sacrificed our usefulness to the profession and the community we serve; students don't learn without hope for a positive outcome. Differentiating teachers keep hope ever present.

So, go ahead—guilt-free—and occasionally adjust the pacing of your curriculum for some students if you think they will learn better. Be brave enough to adjust the standards if necessary to live up to a school's overall goal: to teach students well.

Wait a minute, you think. This sounds like lowering the standards because a kid can't hack it. This is exactly what No Child Left Behind was meant to prevent. We're watering down the curriculum! We're going soft! Students will graduate knowing nothing! What the cynics say about education is true!

Nothing could be further from the truth. In fact, adjusting the standards from time to time to provide developmentally appropriate practices actually increases what students learn and the material for which we can hold them accountable. How so?

If Sam is struggling to find and maintain the correct musical key while singing, we keep coaching him until he can. Other students may be able to sing on key consistently and are ready to focus on singing individual notes with the correct pitch, something more advanced than just maintaining the right key. We move these students forward with lessons on pitch. Adding pitch lessons to Sam's plate right now, however, might overwhelm him. It would dilute his success with both skills, key and pitch, so we hold back. After a few more lessons on identifying and maintaining the correct musical key for a song and his vocal range, we move Sam into the pitch lessons.

These accommodations don't dilute the curriculum for Sam. Adjusting the pacing of the lesson increases what Sam can learn. He would retain less if we threw these musical concepts at him when he wasn't ready to understand them. Some of you who don't know much about singing are thinking right now that you'd be overwhelmed to learn about both key and pitch at the same time. "Let me learn one thing at a time," you plead, regardless of where your classmates might be. This is one of the perennial decisions in a differentiated classroom: Is the student ready to move on, or does he need more time with the current topic or skill? Will moving him on provide the meaningful context for him to learn the current topic better, or will it short-circuit his attempts to learn?

Lowering standards means that we expect some students to fall short of the identified learning goals. This is not what we're doing. The purpose of an effectively differentiated classroom is to push for all students to achieve mastery, though not necessarily in the same way or at the same pace. We might temporarily simplify the requirements for some students, but that does not mean we will eliminate the benchmarks. We'll reinsert those goals as soon as it's developmentally appropriate to do so.

This highlights the role of assessment in the differentiated classroom. We assess students' proficiency, then we adjust our instruction—adding/subtracting/changing elements, increasing/decreasing the pace—based on the data gained from the assessment. Doing this increases students' performance; it does not diminish it. Teachers who do not adjust instructional pacing for struggling or advanced students will cause them to flounder.

Don't forget, too, that once we identify what is most critical to teach, we must consider what we will accept as evidence of mastery. This should involve more than superficial recitation of information to satisfy the teacher. For example, should our students prove only that they can identify adverbs in a paragraph, or should they also show and explain why too many adverbs can weaken writing and how they could substitute stronger verbs for those feeble adverbs? And should they be able to do this consistently throughout the school year?

Consider what you will accept as evidence of mastery as you identify your objectives or outcomes.

Check out the Recommended Resources for some great books that can help you determine objectives, learner outcomes, and benchmarks. You also may wish to consider the following:

- State or province standards of learning

- Programs of study

- Curriculum guides

- Pacing guides

- Other teachers' tests

- Professional journals

- Mentor or colleague teachers
- Textbook scope and sequence
- Textbook end-of-chapter reviews and tests
- Subject-specific email lists
- Benchmarks and standards identified by professional organizations

Take the time to identify what you think is important to teach as well as all the content and skills inherent in those ideas. Then take the time to share your thinking with others who have taught the subject before and ask for their feedback. This back-and-forth exchange will help, but it will take time to conduct these conversations by email, phone calls, or personal visits. You may need a week or more to do this properly.

For the purposes of this example, consider the planning process involved in designing a unit of study about the early explorers of the world. The unit will include information about:

- James Cook
- John Cabot
- Jacques Cartier
- Samuel de Champlain
- Sir John Franklin
- Martin Frobisher
- Henry Hudson
- Vasco da Gama
- Cabeza de Vaca
- Hernando De Soto
- Ferdinand Magellan
- Sir Francis Drake
- Marco Polo
- Leif Ericson
- Amerigo Vespucci
- Hernando Cortéz
- Prince Henry
- Francisco Pizarro
- Vasco de Balboa
- Francisco Coronado
- Sir Walter Raleigh
- Christopher Columbus
- Meriwether Lewis and William Clark
- Ponce de Leon
- Ludwig Leichhardt, Robert O'Hara Burke and William John Wills, Hamilton Hume and William Hovell, Matthew Flinders, George Bass, Edmund Kennedy, John Forrest (all from Australia)

According to the school district's goals for this unit, my students should be able to

1. Identify the early explorer and his contribution to our understanding of the world at the time he lived.

CHAPTER 2: A Walk-Through of a Differentiated Lesson

2. Trace the explorer's routes on a map or globe.

3. Describe the impact of the explorer on the native populations he discovered during his journeys.

4. Explain why countries sent explorers around the world to colonize.

5. Explain the hardships that the explorers endured.

6. Create a time line of exploration.

From my own experience and reading about these explorers, I wanted to add a seventh objective. Students should be able to

7. Explain why our modern society considers it important to know about these early explorers.

In looking at these objectives, notice that the first three goals focus on the individual explorer and the last four on explorers in general. Objectives four and seven, in particular, suggest essential understandings or questions that would create a nice framework for the whole unit.

As you explore differentiated lessons further, keep in mind the following references to help you define the lesson objectives:

- Essential and Enduring Knowledge, also known as EEK, plus what's nice to know (for students who need enrichment)

- Know, Understand, and Do, also known as KUD, as found in Grant Wiggins and Jay McTighe's very helpful *Understanding by Design* books (2004; 2005) and other resources on differentiation.

Essential understandings, i.e. essential and enduring knowledge, usually represent larger framework questions that transcend the unit of study and are not easy to answer. For example, "What makes a culture a civilization?" is an essential question that we can use when exploring the history of Mesopotamia or Egypt. The specific curriculum fits within this broader perspective.

The *Know* in the second reference refers to concepts that are easily memorized, such as the formula for the area of a parallelogram or the date on which a famous battle occurred. *Understand* refers to students' mastery of connections, relationships, and patterns in and across the curriculum, and *Do* refers to specific skill demonstrations and applications.

Both approaches to generating a lesson's objectives or outcomes are worth using. In fact, many educators begin by designing essential understandings or questions, then break them into the three categories of Know, Understand, and Do. Unpacking standards and objectives like this is not

Restate the objectives in your own words.

required in every individual lesson, but it is highly suggested for overall unit planning. The process provides the big-picture perspective as well as the focused skills that keep learning progressing.

The lives of any of the previously mentioned explorers are interesting, but for the purposes of learning how to design a differentiated lesson we'll narrow the focus to Hernando Cortéz (an Americanized spelling of *Hernan Cortés*).

If this is the first time we have taught this unit, we will need time to identify all of the objectives and information about Cortéz. We may confer with colleagues, research information on the Internet, watch some videos, visit museum exhibits, read relevant literature, peruse the materials provided by the school district, and reflect on our own understanding of Cortéz. Only after clarifying the learning objectives and the Cortéz information should we proceed to the next step.

Understand that there will never be enough time to do this every time we teach a new unit. Nevertheless, we can try to complete most of these steps most of the time. Given all that is on our professional plates, we won't always be able to design the perfect unit and respond effectively to all the variables that occur in our daily interactions with students, colleagues, the curriculum, and our families, but we can still push towards the greater goal. Some days we feel tired and cranky and will need to preserve what little energy and motivation are left, tossing good pedagogy to the wind. This is fine; it's normal. But we can't play the defeatist for the whole year and fail to start something for fear of never finishing. Many of our achievements in education and society would never have happened if the majority of us gave in to the daunting nature of our tasks. One day at a time, we can do this, especially if we're not alone. And we are not alone.

Give yourself time to develop differentiation strategies.

As with anything, differentiation gets easier the more you do it. Give yourself three years to become comfortable with it. Try one idea per month, then one per week. Perhaps all you do is complete one thorough lesson per grading period. That's progress.

Identify Those Students Who Have Special Needs, and Start Thinking About How You Will Adapt Your Instruction to Ensure They Can Learn and Achieve

Create and consult learning profiles of your students.

Use whatever informal and formal tools you can to get to know your students. Create a profile for each learner. A learner profile consists of a file that lists every factor you discover about a student that could affect his or her learning, positively and negatively. You might include any of the following factors: preferred learning styles, family poverty or mobility, multiple intelligences, special education labels, musical talents, bipolar disorder, school leadership activities, fetal alcohol syndrome, learned helplessness, quirky sense of humor, a parent serving overseas with the military, academic giftedness, personal interests, nationality, or major events in their lives. See the Recommended Resources for sources of additional ideas.

For the purpose of this sample lesson, let's assume that you have already started compiling this data and have gained a deeper appreciation of your students' strengths and weaknesses. Here's a possible breakdown of your fourth-period class:

Grade Level: Seventh Grade
Total Students: 34 (18 boys, 16 girls)

- Five students have a federal 504 Plan, which means that you must make certain classroom accommodations to guide their learning. For example, one student has an anxiety disorder and can't make public presentations. You let her discuss her findings with you privately. Another student suffers from obsessive-compulsive disorder and often can't complete tests within the required time frame because classroom distractions cause him to endlessly repeat steps. You let him finish exams after school.

- Nine students have documented learning disabilities in reading, writing, and/or language development. You must follow the strategies detailed in each student's Individual Education Plan ("IEP" in the United States).

Describe the unique nature of your students' learning needs.

- Twenty-two students are from other cultures; eight of these students are struggling to learn English, and you suspect that two were prematurely released from the self-contained program to teach them basic English.

- Seven students have been identified as gifted and talented and need advanced standards and varied assignments that will enable them to go deeper into the curriculum.

- Eighteen students qualify for the federal subsidized lunch program, a key indication of family poverty.

- Half the class, both girls and boys, plays basketball almost year round.

- In terms of Howard Gardner's multiple intelligences theory (1983), about half the class has a strong desire to be physically active when learning and a significant percentage of the students respond best to interpersonal exchanges. A few are most comfortable learning independently, and their needs must be addressed as well. You also have several strong artists in the group, including some students who use a detailed graffiti style and some who are skilled at Anime cartooning.

- In addition to the documented disabilities previously mentioned, you know that some of your students have a difficult time concentrating and blocking out distracting stimuli, so you address their needs informally, whether or not they have obtained outside verification of the problems. You focus on what your students need in order to be successful, not just on the accommodations you are legally obligated to provide.

Design Formative and Summative Assessments

Before writing your lessons, write your assessments.

Before you generate the first lesson, have a clear picture in your mind of where you want to end up with your students. You did this initially when you designed your objectives, but that's not enough. Objectives are abstractions until you back them up with details of what you will accept as evidence of mastery.

There are three types of assessments: *Preassessments* occur prior to the creation of our lesson plans; we use these to diagnose students' readiness levels. *Formative assessments* can be conducted throughout the lesson to monitor students' progress and adjust activities as necessary to maximize learning. *Postassessments*—or summative assessments—are used after the lesson or unit to document the skills and concepts students learned. Preassessments are usually "cut-to-the-chase" versions of summative assessments, so we can't create them until we've designed the latter.

Remind yourself of the broader context of your lesson— how does it fit?

The first step is to brainstorm possible ways for students to demonstrate their understanding of the objectives. Let's list these objectives again for reference.

1. Identify the early explorer and his contribution to our understanding of the world at the time he lived.

2. Trace the explorer's routes on a map or globe.

3. Describe the impact of the explorer on the native populations he discovered during his journeys.

4. Explain why countries sent explorers around the world to colonize.

5. Explain the hardships that the explorers endured.

6. Create a time line of exploration.

7. Explain why our modern society considers it important to know about these early explorers.

Brainstorm your assessments.

Remember, too, that Cortéz is only one of thirty-four explorers on the list. As you brainstorm, think about assessments that will demonstrate understanding of individual explorers as well as how to assess students' knowledge of the explorers as a group, distinguishing one from another.

Don't worry about whether the assessments are summative or formative at this point. Just list them. Here are some suggestions:

- Given a description of an early explorer, students can correctly identify Cortéz.

- Given the name "Cortéz," students can correctly describe his explorations and explain his importance to history.

- Compare and contrast Cortéz with two other early explorers. Demonstrate at least two similarities and two differences between Cortéz and each explorer, using evidence from the text and videos from the unit.

- Test question: "Identify and explain at least three contributions Cortéz made to our understanding of the world, and identify the years in which he made these contributions."

- Given a blank map, students can trace and label Cortéz's journeys.

- Test question: "What impact did Cortéz have on the Aztecs, and how do we know this?"

- Test question: "Identify and explain at least three hardships that Cortéz and his men suffered during their expeditions."

- Test question: "Why should we care about what Cortéz did so many years ago? What relevance do his explorations have to today's world?"

Now that we've brainstormed some possibilities for assessment, look back at the objectives list. Did we include everything? It seems so. Will these formats enable all students to accurately communicate what they know? Perhaps. We may need to assess some of these orally instead of through writing. We may need to let some of the students represent their knowledge artistically. We will see how things develop and not be wedded to a "my-way-or-the-highway" mentality.

Compare your assessments with your objectives— have you accounted for everything?

Design and Deliver Preassessments Based on Summative Assessments and Identified Objectives

For preassessments, we can look at our summative assessments and pull out little pieces. Here are some simple preassessments for this unit that might work:

From your summative assessments, determine your preassessments.

Ask students to provide short responses to the following questions:

- Who was Hernando Cortéz, and what did he do for the world?

- How did Cortéz impact the Aztecs?

- Compare Cortéz with one other explorer.

- What hardships did Cortéz's army have to endure?

- What can we learn from studying the early explorers?

Would we do this for all thirty-four explorers? Probably not, though it's not out of the question. We might do so for the major world navigators, or we could simply create a chart like the one in Figure 2.2 and ask students to fill in the boxes as best they can, leaving the more general objectives (such as number 7 about why modern students study early explorers) in the

FIGURE 2.2 Sample Preassessment for Early Explorers

Explorer	Time Period	Contributions	Impact	Hardships
Balboa				
Cartier				
Cook				
Cortéz				
Drake				
Magellan				
Pizarro				

question form suggested above. The explorers could be grouped according to geographic region, nationality, or the periods in which they lived.

After conducting the preassessments, we can begin to group students according to their understanding of each standard or outcome. At a minimum, consider placing students in groups of those on grade level and those above grade level. If, after preassessing students, you discover that one or more students are significantly below grade level, create a group for them as well. Don't assume that there will be high, medium, and low groups in every situation. It's much wiser to respond to what you have in front of you. For instance, you may have a class in which the majority of students operate at a very high level of understanding, or one with students clustered at a very low level, with just a few students at grade level.

Important note: It's very hard to analyze preassessment data and design appropriate, differentiated lessons based on that data after a long day of teaching. Try to preassess about a week ahead of the first day of a new unit so you have sufficient time to analyze the data and create effective differentiated lessons, implementing them on the first day. Do yourself this favor. If you plan to start your early explorers unit on Monday, make sure to give the preassessment during class or as a take-home assignment on Monday or Tuesday of the previous week.

Complete the pre-assessments before the first day of the new unit.

By this point, you should have plenty to write in the margins to remind yourself of the steps for designing a real differentiated lesson on your own. Go back and review some of the sections and record quick notes that identify these specific steps. Examples of notes to record here in the margins include, "Brainstorm potential assessments," "Check the objectives again," "Figure out how my students learn differently," and "Preassessments are smaller chunks broken off the summative assessments." Write whatever notes help you remember the sequence of steps, and refer to the printed notes in boxes in the margins as well.

Adjust Assessments and Objectives Based on Further Thinking While Designing Assessments

One of the assessments suggested previously deals with comparing and contrasting.

> "Compare and contrast Cortéz with two other early explorers.
> Demonstrate at least two similarities and two differences between
> Cortéz and each explorer, using evidence from the text and videos
> from the unit."

This seemed important to include because, with so many explorers to consider, students might get confused about who is who. In *Habits of Mind* (2000), Art Costa and Bena Kallick encourage teachers in all subject disciplines to help students discern similarities and differences among concepts and people. This is a perfect place to reflect these ideas. We need to add this emphasis to the list of objectives. Let's record it as:

Compare and contrast the explorer with at least two other explorers in terms of contributions, impact, and/or hardships endured.

Be open to revising your objectives and assessments as you plan.

Now let's go back and rewrite the summative assessment prompt as follows (italics indicate additions):

"Compare and contrast Cortéz with two other early explorers *in terms of contributions, impact, and/or hardships endured.* Demonstrate at least two similarities and two differences between Cortéz and each explorer, using evidence from the text and videos from the unit."

This revision links our summative assessments to our goals. Now, let's move to the formative assessments.

Once again, we can use parts of the summative assessments to create our formative assessments. Usually these will be quick checks that show us how students are learning and help us provide useful feedback about their progress. Formative assessments should be efficient for our benefit as well. Some possibilities include:

- Match the explorer to his description.

- Identify two differences between Cortéz and Pizarro.

- Identify two similarities between Cortéz and Pizarro.

- Pictionary (Without using words or numerals, students draw pictures, clues, and symbols to help their teammates guess the correct explorer or topic.)

- Charades (Without speaking, students use gestures and pantomime to help their teammates guess the correct explorer or topic.)

- Taboo (Students design decks of cards. Each card includes a heading, such as an explorer's name or a major exploration, and five words commonly associated with the name or topic. Teams exchange decks of cards. Without mentioning any of the "taboo" words listed underneath, representatives from each team must try to get their peers to identify the correct heading of each card. Using a one- or two-minute timer, teams accumulate as many correct responses as possible within the deadline. Each correct response earns the team one point. If the team uses a taboo word, the card and its point go to the opposing team.

- Draw Cortéz's routes on a blank map.

- Trace Cortéz's route with your finger on a globe.

- Draw a time line of several explorers' major expeditions.

- Identify at least one impact that Cortéz had on the Aztec people.

- Portray a hardship endured by Cortéz's army that differed from the experiences of Christopher Columbus.

- How does what we've learned about this explorer help us understand today's politics?

- Explain the statement, "History is often written by the victors." Consider what implications this statement could have for our modern society looking to the future.

We've now explored the steps differentiating teachers take to prepare for writing their lesson plans, also known as learning experiences. Let's remind ourselves of those steps:

1. Identify what we have to teach (our objectives).

2. Figure out how our students are different from one another and how they best learn.

3. Create our assessments, starting with the final, summative assessment and including many ideas for preassessments and formative assessments.

4. Conduct the preassessments for the unit or lesson, then contemplate the results and what the data mean for adjusting the learning experiences.

5. Double-check our assessments against the learning objectives and make adjustments to keep them correlated.

Now we're ready to design and prepare the experiences necessary for *all* our students to learn: our lesson plans.

Steps to Take *While* Designing and Implementing the Learning Experiences

As you may recall from the lesson design sequence, the first step at this stage is: "Design the learning experiences for students based on the information gathered from those preassessments; your knowledge of your students; and your expertise with the curriculum, cognitive theory, and students at this stage of human development." We are ready to create actual lesson plans.

Our mind-set as we design our lessons is: *Given these objectives, the varied needs of my students, and the assessments that I've selected, what learning experiences will ensure that every student will learn the curriculum well?* Or, in terms of testing, *. . . will earn a perfect score on every assessment?*

The goal is success for all students, no matter which paths they take. If students don't achieve as expected, we will analyze our practices, revise, and reteach them in other ways until they master the skills.

Notice how this mind-set differs from unhelpful approaches to instruction such as: *Here is the lesson. After students complete all the activities in the unit, we will see how they compare against the yardstick of achievement. If they don't reach the top, they will just have to work harder next time, and if they're bored because they already know it, they'll have to learn patience because that's what we need in this world.*

This alternative view focuses on justification—being able to claim that we "covered" the curriculum as directed. When we do this, we shift all the blame for failure to students and refuse to consider how our classroom practices directly affect their ability to learn. In contrast, teachers who differentiate know they play a central role in students' achievement. Mindful of the need to make these critical connections, they adopt a variety of approaches to ensure they will be able to provide what all students need to excel.

Before we get too far into specific lesson design, let's remember those very important steps that help us move forward in our planning and implementation of differentiated lessons:

- Run a mental tape of each step in the lesson sequence to make sure that the process makes sense for your diverse group of students and will help the lesson run smoothly.

- Review your plans with a colleague.

- Obtain/create materials needed for the lesson.

- Conduct the lesson.

- Adjust formative and summative assessments and objectives as necessary based on observations and data collected while teaching the lessons.

Because teachers typically follow this sequence during instruction, I won't elaborate on the individual elements here. The primary focus in this section will be the actual lesson plan. However, you may want to stop periodically throughout the planning process and anticipate problems: Will students have enough supplies? Will it be too noisy for some students?

Will everyone get a chance to share their thinking? Where will you stand at that pivotal moment in the lesson? Have you accounted for as many of the "What if?" variables as possible? Also try to review your plans with a trusted colleague. As you settle on definite tasks and experiences for students, start gathering the necessary materials. And don't be afraid to adjust your goals or assessments based on new insights gained while planning and implementing your lessons. I'll throw in a few reminders of these steps while discussing the lesson ahead.

Brainstorm Potential Strategies or Learning Experiences

At first, we may be dumbfounded by the task: *How do I come up with varied ideas for teaching the same thing?* The best advice is to start with a solid architectural framework and fill in the blueprints over time. Initially, try to concentrate on brainstorming, not perfecting, practices. Don't worry about adopting the ideal sequence of learning, either; you can do that later.

If you're stuck for ideas, consider consulting colleagues in person or by email; asking for ideas through a professional listserv dedicated to your discipline; engaging in some outside reading on the subject or the particular teaching strategies; reviewing the suggestions listed in the teacher's edition of the basal text; quietly reflecting for thirty minutes or more (a lost art); or asking students for advice—they often know what it takes for them to learn!

Figure 2.3 provides a possible list of strategies that you could use for this unit. Many of the strategies would make great assessment ideas as well. Include in such lists everything you can think of, even strategies you've listed before.

If you're like me, you'll eventually come up with dozens of ideas as you plan. At some moment, however, you'll look over the learning objectives and all the strategies you've brainstormed and realize you've created something that is much more than a simple differentiated lesson or two—it's a whole unit of study! This happens almost every time to every teacher who differentiates; it's normal.

We often start out planning a single day's lesson plan but we overdo it and have to decide whether or not to make the lesson into something longer, given the scope of our teaching goals and ideas on how to teach them. An important aspect of our planning is how each lesson fits within the larger whole. Don't be afraid to overplan; the process can provide lesson context and instructional dexterity: we know where students are coming from and where they are going, and we can be flexible with instruction because we have many choices for how to proceed with the whole group or with subgroups within the class.

As you read the examples that follow, be aware that some of the activities cited for one lesson's use may take two or three days to complete. In addition, I have offered multiple ideas because subgroups may be involved

FIGURE 2.3 Brainstormed Strategies for Unit on Cortéz

Unless otherwise noted, the names of specific resources listed here are imaginary. They are included for sample purposes only.

- Read pages 86 to 102 in the textbook, *The Early World*.
- Read a different interpretation of the same information, using a second textbook, specifically pages 33 to 51 in *Civilization on the Rise*. Compare the two versions.
- Ask students to create decks of Taboo playing cards, based on the explorers from our unit. Let them play the game.
- "Snow globe" Cortéz. This is an actual metaphor suggested by Kelly Gallagher in his wonderful book *Deeper Reading*. A tourist's snow globe of a favorite site usually portrays the salient features of that location. What would students consider essential to include in Cortéz's snow globe?
- Watch the film *Cortéz and the Aztecs*.
- Give students a copy of the test on the first day of the unit so they can use it as a study guide—be sure to teach them how to use it as a study guide.
- Refer back to Figure 2.2, the explorers' chart that we used as part of the preassessment of this unit. Revise as we learn more information about each explorer.
- Exit card ideas: Identify two similarities and two differences between Cortéz and Pizarro. Identify an impact of Cortéz on the Aztec people.
- Play Pictionary by having students draw clues and have their classmates guess the correct explorer or topic.
- Play charades by having students use gestures and pantomime to help their classmates guess the correct explorer or topic.
- Play the "Who Am I?" game in which students portray various explorers and ask their classmates to guess their identities.
- More than once, draw a time line of several explorers' major expeditions. In addition to writing or drawing this, students can create a time line using a rope strung from two points in the classroom; students place large index cards, folded like tents, containing the names of different explorers in the correct chronological order along the rope.
- Ask students to dramatize Cortéz's interactions with the Aztecs. One group can take the point of view of the invaders, and another group can reflect the native population's perspective. Afterward, debate the different interpretations.
- Class discussion: How does our knowledge of early explorers help us understand today's politics and the rules of engagement during war with other nations? With immigration laws?
- Class discussion: What does this unit on early explorers help us understand about imperialism and "Manifest Destiny"?
- Lecture on the impact that the early explorers had on the native populations.
- Class discussion followed by learning log reflection: "History is often written by the victors."
- Formal debate or panel discussion: Explorers' lasting impact on early civilizations.
- Engage in some role-playing exercises with the students in which they depict the explorer's journey using the education simulations, "Discovery," "Explorers," and "Maya" modules from Interact. (See actual simulations at www.teachinteract.com.)
- Visit the website "Explorers: Fact or Fiction?" and

Notice that some of these assessment ideas make great teaching strategies as well.

with different strategies at the same time, but no one group will complete all the activities (learning experiences). We want to be prepared for varied learners. If you really like an idea but don't get to use it this year, use it when you teach the unit again. Aim for the single day's lesson, but keep in mind that it's part of a larger unit of study.

Also, remember to keep all of your strategies in one running list. Some of the ideas for preassessments and summative assessments listed in the first section, for example, are listed in the strategies section below as well. That's by design: assessments are learning experiences, so this is a natural-

ask students to complete a survey to see if they can separate fact from fiction.

- Show a portfolio of drawings of Cortéz's journey borrowed from the Early Empires exhibit at the Smithsonian Institution, and ask students to analyze the depictions in terms of the hardships the explorer had to endure.
- Read and analyze the letters Cortéz and his army wrote, as presented in the "Primary Documents" section of the CD-ROM that came with the basal textbook.
- Complete a WebQuest about Cortéz and the impact of the explorers on the people and lands they explored. A WebQuest is a real activity teachers use regularly. It's a research project that shows students how to *use* information found on the Internet, rather than simply *locating* online resources. It helps them to develop their creative-thinking and problem-solving skills.
- Ask students to read one book about the Aztecs and their interpretation of Cortéz's armies.
- Invite someone of authority to come into the classroom and tell us that our way of conducting class is unacceptable. Then have that person impose new and strange rules for how we should teach and learn and list the consequences for failing to comply. Make sure that the visitor claims that these procedures are based on his or her faith, which won't be familiar to us or students. For dramatic emphasis, make sure that the invader tears down a poster or two (something of little value we've previously posted just for this purpose). Ask the visitor to remove any obvious valuables from the room before leaving. We need to keep a straight face and pretend this demonstration is real. When the invader moves on to another classroom, we will ask the students what they are feeling and what we should do in response.
- Play Concentration with cards of the explorers, matching descriptions to names.
- Provide multiple practice sessions with blank maps, drawing and labeling Cortéz's routes.
- Ask students to describe a scene from Cortéz's exploration by trying to emulate Cortéz's writing and perspective.
- Ask students to describe the same scene, but this time through the perspective of the Aztec people and their collective writer's voice.
- Ask students to create flash cards to be used when practicing and playing Explorer Rummy, following the rules of the traditional card game but using different patterns: Spanish explorers (or any other heritage); explorers who suffered from scurvy; explorers who found sailing passages through or around difficult areas; explorers who were sponsored by countries instead of private financiers; explorers who in retrospect did more harm than good; explorers whose discoveries led to improvements in science or medicine, and so on.
- Class discussion: How are we different today because of Cortéz's explorations?
- Ask students to ask their parents, a school board member, or a curriculum developer why Cortéz and the early explorers are part of the mandated curriculum. If possible, invite a school board member to come to the classroom and explain the rationale. Invite an archeologist or museum director to come to the classroom to explain his or her take on the same question.

ly occurring part of our planning. In fact, if we didn't include assessments in our instructional strategies, I would worry. It would be a sign that we were limiting our lesson brainstorming. We want everything in one place so we have an easy reference.

As we create these learning experiences in our lessons, we also want to constantly reference the objectives to see if we've captured all the critical points and have approached instruction from a variety of angles, including providing more than one level of complexity and reflecting multiple stages of readiness. This is an oscillating process; we will want to move back and forth between the standards and the assessments, the preassessments and the daily lesson plan, and so on. Ultimately we want to move in one direction—toward student success.

Some readers will look at the list in Figure 2.3 and wonder whether or not I've lost my mind. There's no way any one teacher can use all of these activities in a single unit of study. You'd have to devote five weeks to Cortéz alone and you'd still have thirty-three explorers to teach, plus the rest of the curriculum.

Just brainstorm strategies. Cluster them for complexity later.

Don't worry. You're not compiling this list to make every moment of the school day a sprint. You're making the list to increase your teaching dexterity so you can meet the diverse needs of your students. You will want to start arranging these activities in clusters of readiness levels (complexity), but you can't possibly attend to everything on the list. You may decide to try some of the strategies initially and see how effective they are with your students. If these ideas don't work, try others. Or you may find that some techniques are most effective with certain groups of students. If a strategy works and students learn the material solidly, you can save the rest of the activities for other units or next year's students.

Brainstorming strategies isn't just a nice activity to do if we have time. With a large repertoire of responses, we can respond immediately to the students before us. We can't move as deftly unless we have a big "drop-down" menu of options prepared in advance. Truly, 90 percent of differentiated instruction is what we do before students walk through our classroom doors.

To illustrate the point, imagine being three days into the unit on the early explorers and discovering that the majority of the class remains as clueless as a wayward navigator. You may be tempted to tell the advanced students to work on some puzzles in the back of the classroom while they wait for their peers to catch up, or you may ask them to help struggling classmates, read quietly, straighten up the bookshelves, or complete homework for another class. Although you might occasionally allow these activities, none of them should be your standard default response. It's disrespectful to students to force them to spin their wheels while the rest of the class tries to accelerate. It's also developmentally inappropriate, and differentiation is doing what is developmentally appropriate.

Plan so well that you can go in different directions as needed.

When we do the footwork to design multiple approaches to teaching a topic, we have flexibility. If some students are excelling, we move past the introductory tasks to the more advanced tasks—perhaps offering them more autonomy, more factors to consider, unusual comparisons to make, the chance to reframe the topic under a different theme or to apply the ideas to the world beyond school. If some students are struggling, we allow the rest of the class to move forward while we provide more foundational, introductory experiences for these students until they, too, are ready to move forward. This adjusting for varied students' readiness is called "tiering." For further thinking on tiering, see Chapter 3.

You may wonder if you can have a life while providing differentiated instruction for thirty to 180 students. It's true that it takes time to generate new ideas, such as those on the brainstorming list. Planning and preparing all those activities might take a week or two more. But in truth, you will have more time when you differentiate than when you do not.

First, students learn better and faster the first time around when we differentiate as it's warranted. When we constantly present standardized instruction, there will always be students who fall behind and require extended remediation before, during, and after school, as well as after the final exam. They learn inaccurately in nondifferentiated lessons. Then they practice the incorrect information, and practice makes permanent. We have to go back and undo the misinterpretations—a difficult and not always successful process—then take the time to teach the students the material correctly. When we differentiate for successful learning, however, most students will absorb the correct concepts efficiently. The time we would have spent on remediation and reorientation can be used for other things.

By the way, this includes not giving students homework assignments to practice something unless we've used a formal or informal assessment to make sure students completely understand the concept. Homework won't compensate for ineffective instruction. It will confuse the kids who didn't understand the lesson and bore the ones who did get the main ideas unless we match the practice to their level of understanding.

Second, when we initially design a differentiated unit, we will invest a significant amount of time; there's no sugarcoating that point. In general, I've spent about two hours on three different occasions during the week, plus half a day on the weekend to design a three- or four-week unit with differentiated lessons, activities, and assessments. That's a lot of time. But fine-tuning my footwork in the initial planning stages enables me to deftly move in various directions based on the needs of my students. The second time I teach that unit, I can have a satisfying life outside of school. In the middle of the week I can take my wife out to dinner, exercise, and even read for enjoyment—previously unobtainable dreams. I just tweak the lessons in a few places to address varied students' needs or to incorporate new information or additional strategies.

One last thing: It took me about twenty minutes to assemble the list of teaching strategies in Figure 2.3. That's a relatively short time to come up with so many ideas. How does that happen? Practice and more practice. I've been using differentiated teaching to varying degrees for more than twenty-five years. The process has become almost as automatic as breathing. But I didn't start out that way.

Experience really helps. Every time we do a differentiated lesson it gets a little easier to do the next one. Multiple effective approaches reside in our mental fingertips, ready to be used real-time in the classroom, as we need them. We don't have to wait and go look them up after school or over the summer.

As we differentiate, we become much more aware of dozens of resources to which we can turn when we are stuck, and we get better at asking others to brainstorm with us. Discussions with colleagues can help us create comprehensive lists, such as the one in Figure 2.3.

I remember one school year when I was struggling to get my students to work in groups of five or six for any significant time. They just wouldn't or couldn't cooperate, and nothing I tried seemed to work. I mentioned this problem one day to the reading specialist in my school, and she reminded me to start with small steps. She said that I should pair my students for a task that only took five minutes and be very direct and structured about what they were to do—there should be no wiggle room. Once they had completed these tasks several times, I could expand the task while giving them slightly more autonomy. Along the way, my colleague suggested, I would need to provide a lot of feedback to my students so they would know exactly what I wanted and how close they were to meeting the goals. After that, she told me, I could combine pairs into groups of four students to complete a task that at first was more structured, then later was more open-ended. Eventually I could engage up to six students in a group, each working together on a task for about thirty minutes without me hovering like a helicopter to keep them on task.

This idea of starting very small and teacher-directed and moving towards something large and student-directed, all while providing ample feedback, was the epiphany I needed. It kick-started my evolution into a teacher who could effectively scaffold instruction. Now the process works beautifully every time I use it.

This conversation with the reading specialist took place in 1990, after I had already been teaching for almost a decade. I shudder to think of all the students whose needs might not have been addressed because I was ready to drop small-group work for lack of effectiveness. Scaffolding is a simple, straightforward instructional idea, but I wasn't able to understand what it required until I discussed my weakness with my insightful colleague.

Cluster Strategies into Introductory Through Advanced Experiences

As we take the next steps in our planning process, we will return to the strategies in our differentiated unit, this time clustering them according to complexity—some introductory, some intermediate, and some advanced. Figure 2.4 provides this newly clustered list. I've abbreviated the descriptions to make it easier to see the clusters. The activities are listed according to relative challenge or complexity, which is the critical next step in our thinking.

FIGURE 2.4 Brainstormed Strategy List Clustered According to Complexity

Introductory Readiness Level

- Give students a copy of the test.
- Intruder visit.
- Pages 86 to 102, *The Early World*
- Read a different interpretation pages 33 to 51, *Civilization on the Rise*, compare the two.
- Film, *Cortéz and the Aztecs.*
- Revise the explorers chart.
- Exit card: Identify two differences and two similarities between Cortéz and Pizarro.
- Exit card: Identify an impact of Cortéz on the Aztec people.
- "Who Am I?" game.
- Pictionary.
- Charades.
- Practice drawing a time line of explorers' expeditions. Use rope and hanging tent cards for time line sequence, too.
- Lecture.
- Visit the website "Explorers: Fact or Fiction?," complete the survey.
- Concentration game.
- Draw Cortéz's routes.
- Explorer flash cards for practice and Rummy.

Intermediate Readiness Level

- Portfolio of Cortéz's journey from Smithsonian Institution, analyze hardships.
- Role play explorer's journey via simulations.
- Through fine or performing arts, ask students to portray a hardship endured.

- Play Taboo.
- WebQuest.
- Students read one book on the Aztecs and their interpretation of Cortéz's armies.
- Play Explorer Rummy.

Advanced Readiness Level

- Students ask others why Cortéz and the early explorers are part of the mandated curriculum.
- Invite archeologist or museum director to explain his or her take on the same question.
- Describe a scene from Cortéz exploration days through Cortéz's perspective.
- Describe same scene but via the perspective of the Aztec people.
- Conduct formal debate: pros and cons of explorers' impact.
- Class discussion: How are we different today because of Cortéz?
- Class discussion: What does this information have to do with today's politics?
- Class discussion: What does this have to do with imperialism and "Manifest Destiny"?
- Class discussion and learning log reflection: Explain, "History is often written by the victors" and what it means for teachers and students, and for our future.
- Read and analyze the letters written by Cortéz and members of his party.
- Create collages that "snow globe" Cortéz.

Double-Check That Strategies Meet the Needs of Exceptional Students and Learning Objectives

After we've gone back through the state standards, learner outcomes, or objectives to make sure we've reflected a variety of angles, we have one more calibration to make—correlate the strategies with the composition of each class. We were mindful of students' different strengths and preferences when we developed the list. We included activities to get them moving, talking, listening, reading, and more. But let's double-check just to be

Recheck the class description to make sure the strategies match students' needs.

sure. As you may recall, we have students in our representative class who are

- Into Anime cartooning
- Under a 504 plan
- Learning disabled in language arts
- Nonnative English speakers
- Gifted/talented/advanced
- Living in poverty
- Avid basketball players

We don't want to lose sight of these students as we design our lessons. Brainstorming some possible responses to their needs keeps us focused. To meet these students' needs, how about adding the following options to our plan?

- Ask some students to create short, graphic comic novels of Cortéz's interactions with the Aztecs.

- Pair nonnative speakers with students who have strong literacy skills and let them practice reading aloud.

- Give extended time and extra examples to students who have language gaps and learning disabilities.

- Let some students use graphic organizers to help them make visual connections among new ideas.

- Allow some students, particularly those with advanced knowledge and interest in the subject, to do "orbital" studies (Hollas 2005), choosing one subtopic from the unit to investigate on their own and report back to the class.

- The Aztecs and Mayans played several sports, one of which resembled the game of basketball. Ask the basketball-focused students to research this historical activity and recreate one of the Aztec game courts and explain the rules. Be careful: These games were often played to the death, not just to determine a winner.

- Try to ensure that none of the activities requires extra supplies. If that's not possible, discretely find outside funds for students who can't afford to purchase the supplies.

As you read the list above, you may notice that I provided only one differentiated experience for each of the seven exceptional student categories listed. This wouldn't suffice in a real classroom, of course, as one strategy rarely meets all the needs of a diverse learner. The purpose here is to remind us to take that extra correlation step: We look for the students with truly unique learning needs, and we try to adjust our instruction accordingly.

So here we are. We've been talking about the thinking behind our lesson plans up to this point. Here's another recap of the process so far.

Actions We Take Prior to Lesson Planning

1. Identify what we have to teach (our objectives).

2. Figure out how our students are different from one another and how they best learn.

3. Create our assessments, starting with the final, summative assessment and including many ideas for both preassessments and formative assessments.

4. Conduct the preassessments for the unit or lesson, then contemplate the results and what the data means for adjusting the learning experiences.

5. Double-check our assessments against the learning objectives and make adjustments to keep them correlated.

Actions We Take While Lesson Planning

1. Given what we've discovered about students' learning needs, our lesson's objectives, and the assessments we will give, we brainstorm potential strategies or learning experiences we can provide students so they will be successful.

2. Cluster these strategies into introductory experiences through more advanced experiences to get a rough sequence of learning and to more efficiently match the experiences to learner needs.

3. Double-check that the strategies meet all the needs of exceptional students and the learning objectives.

Sequence the Strategies and Teach the Lesson

Now we're ready to develop the actual sequence for the lessons. The list of strategies clustered by complexity and the short list for some of the unique needs of our students can be saved on our computer or printed as a hard copy and stapled to our lesson-plan book. But we will want to frequently reference these lists as we arrange items in our lesson plans, so we need to make them accessible.

As mentioned earlier, brainstorming for one lesson can lead to a whole unit of ideas. We've done that here. So, as we move ahead, let's narrow the focus to just a portion of what we've brainstormed for the larger unit—something for just a one- or two-day lesson. The procedures for designing and executing this lesson will be the same no matter which portion of the unit we choose. For the purposes of this example, then, let's choose a lesson from the middle of the sequence: Cortéz's impact on the Aztecs.

SAMPLE LESSON

"The Impact of Cortéz on the Aztecs"

Here's what you might write in the dated square of your lesson planner:

> *"Cortéz's Impact"*
> 1. *Surprise invader bursts in, announces new rules—discuss*
> 2. *Brnstrm benefits/damage of conqueror*
> 3. *Video <u>Cortéz and the Aztecs</u> i.d. pos/neg impact and rationale*
> 4. *5 other sources—determine other perspectives on Cortéz*
> 5. *(If time) writer's voice scenes*
> 6. *Written summary, small groups*

Here's the lesson in detail:

Focus

The Impact of Cortéz on the Aztecs

Specific Objectives

- As a result of this lesson, students will be able to explain the impact Cortéz had on the Aztecs from two perspectives: the view of the explorers and the view of the native population.

- Students will be able to explain why it's important to consider different viewpoints when studying historical events.

Assessment

On an exit card (see page 69 for more information about this type of assessment), students will:

1. Identify two or more ways that Cortéz and the Aztecs differed in their interpretations of the invasion.

2. Explain why it's important to consider multiple perspectives when studying historical figures and events.

Materials

- A volunteer, such as a principal, a parent, or a business leader, who will march into the classroom, declare illogical rules that must be followed, and remove valuable items from the classroom.

- A copy of the video *Cortéz and the Aztecs* and the equipment needed to show it.

- The explorers' charts students filled out earlier (Figure 2.2), page 28.

Learning Experiences and Sequence

This is the general lesson *without* any differentiation. It identifies a goal and the itinerary for the class period. The specific ways you might modify the lesson to meet the needs of diverse students will be listed together following this general lesson. Read through the lesson carefully so you will understand the procedures and intent. This review will provide the foundation for the differentiated approaches described.

Also, keep in mind that you don't have to go into such detail with every single lesson. If you did, you might give up teaching, move to an obscure canyon in the wilderness, and grow colorful vegetation. The point of providing so much detail is making the implicit explicit for those who want a behind-the-scenes look at differentiated lesson design. Much of this work will become second nature and you will be able to develop impromptu responses and activities as you gain more experience with differentiation.

A. Introduction/Hook

Begin by asking students to get out their notebooks in preparation for watching a movie. As they do, the volunteer invader comes into class. The invader (an off-duty colleague, a parent, an administrator, a retiree, a custodian, a librarian, or perhaps an employee of a local business partnering with the school), decrees the following:

> Please put down your pencils and clear your desks. This class is under new rule, and the school is under new authority. The way you've been conducting lessons in this room is unacceptable. From now on, you will learn the following ways [*Invader reads from list*]:

- You will not watch any videos or DVDs, nor will you use anything that has an on-switch or a screen.

- You will never doodle on paper or any other surface.

- All books that you read must now and forever focus on how to respect your elders.

- You will dress only in orange clothing. Anything not orange must be burned.

- You will study only the Aztec calendar and the Aztec system of mathematics.

- You will no longer celebrate birthdays. Instead, you will celebrate the beginning of each season of O-whon-tu, which begins every 433 days.

- All of your current religious and community rituals are forbidden.

- You shall spend ninety minutes each evening attending worship services here at the school and twice that many minutes on Saturday morning.

- Whenever someone says the word *pencil* you must fall to your knees, raise your hands over your head, and shout, "Oh, Ticonderoga!"

- You will listen only to the music chosen by a music control board now established in this community.

- You may no longer play any sports.

- When you grow up, your jobs will be chosen for you.

- One half of your wages for the rest of your life will be used to service the god, Mishi.

- You may not share any stories from your childhood with others.

- You will only eat a vegetarian diet.

These posters [*invader grabs a couple of posters put up earlier just for this purpose*] are inappropriate and not pleasing to the god of my faith. [*Invader wads them up and throws them in the trash.*] Never display them again. Also, you may not have anything of value in this room, such as this computer. [*Invader takes some part of it away.*]

These are true and proper procedures based on the newly established religion of this community. Anyone who does not follow these procedures will be locked in a penitentiary for eighteen months. If you break one of the rules a second time, you will forfeit your life. Now continue your lessons, and don't make me come here again. [*Invader leaves the room.*]

After the invader departs, ask the students: "Imagine this is for real. What would you be feeling right now? What would you recommend that we do in response to these mandates? Do you think the majority of the school and community will go along with these new rules because they fear the consequences? If we followed these rules, what would our communities be like fifty years from now?"

B. Identifying the Learning Goal(s) and Priming and Gathering Knowledge

Explain to students that today they will focus on the impact that Cortéz's invasion had on the Aztec people. Ask them to form small groups and brainstorm different ways that an invading force might benefit a native population. Then ask them to consider how the invaders might hurt a conquered people. This is priming students' minds for what's to come.

Next, ask students to watch the twelve-minute video, *Cortéz and the Aztecs,* and note at least five ways Cortéz and his army affected the lives of the Aztec people. Ask students to identify each impact as positive or negative and to explain their thinking.

C. Applying Our Knowledge

Remind students that there is usually more than one perspective about historical events. Ask students to read or examine each of five different descriptions of Cortéz and his impact on students:

- Pages 121 to 123 in the basal text.

- Painting of Cortéz interacting with the Aztecs on one of their farms.

- Photocopied excerpt from a book about Spanish conquistadors.

- Photocopied translation of a letter from one of Cortéz's soldiers to his family explaining what they were doing with the Aztecs.

- Photocopied translation of Aztec oral records of events that transpired during Cortéz's visits.

Ask students to identify subtle and overt differences in the opinions of Cortéz and the Aztecs as portrayed in each example. Next, ask students to consider why we need to read and consider all of these perspectives before forming our own opinions about Cortéz or the Aztecs.

If time allows, select a scene from one of the resources and ask students to describe it, first writing in the voice of Cortéz and secondly from the perspective of the Aztecs.

D. Summary/Closure

Ask students to work with a partner as they write a summary paragraph of no more than eight sentences indicating what they believe to be Cortéz's impact on the Aztecs. Then ask different partner teams to share what they have written with each other. Students should critique each other's summaries for accuracy and evidence to support their claims.

Ask students to create exit cards. Have them take out a half sheet of paper and list two or more ways that Cortéz and the Aztecs differed in their opinions of the invasion. In addition, ask students to reflect on the importance of considering historical figures and events from the perspective of both the conqueror and the conquered.

E. Practice/Homework

Ask students to identify another historical event in which a country or an explorer invaded a territory and seized control. Compare the event to Cortéz's interactions with the Aztecs.

[or]

Ask students to identify any current news event of interest. Once they have identified the topic, students should interpret the event from the perspective of an archeologist 1,000 years into the future. Students must generate at least two different interpretations of what happened and provide supporting evidence. This can be created through writing, artwork, or performance, according to the nature of students in the class. For inspiration, read aloud selections from David Macaulay's wonderful book, *Motel of the Mysteries* (1979).

Differentiation Alternatives for Each Part

Part A

Some students will respond to the visitor's pronouncements calmly, but some may get overexcited or unnerved by the loud decrees. Consider telling these students about the visitor in advance so they won't be startled.

Part B

- When brainstorming how a conqueror benefits or hurts a conquered people, suggest that each group use a T-Chart, if they can't think of a better structure. Allow some students to draw symbols or quick pictures of the benefits/problems, if appropriate (students interested in Anime, for example).

- For students who prefer intrapersonal relationships (from Gardner's multiple intelligences theory), let them complete the list on their own before sharing with the small group.

- For students who will have a difficult time identifying the impact of an invasion, share examples from leadership/government, religion, money, medicine, economy, labor, customs, music, and art. Make sure that all students know what it means to have an impact (to change something in some way).

- For students who will need help staying focused and structuring their responses during the video presentation, provide a graphic organizer such as the one in Figure 2.5.

FIGURE 2.5 Graphic Organizer

1. Impact of Cortéz and his army on the Aztec people: Was this positive or negative? Explain your thinking:
2. Impact of Cortéz and his army on the Aztec people: Was this positive or negative? Explain your thinking:
3. Impact of Cortéz and his army on the Aztec people: Was this positive or negative? Explain your thinking:
4. Impact of Cortéz and his army on the Aztec people: Was this positive or negative? Explain your thinking:
5. Impact of Cortéz and his army on the Aztec people: Was this positive or negative? Explain your thinking:

Part C

- For some classes/students, use a think-aloud activity with one of the five resources they are supposed to examine for different perspectives about Cortéz's invasion. Pretend that you are a student searching for evidence of the artist or author's feelings about Cortéz. Identify the types of attributes you want students to use. Examples: harsh versus encouraging words, darker versus lighter colors, violent versus peaceful images, specific examples used to support claims, what is not described or portrayed versus what is, whether Cortéz figures prominently in the version or not, and so on. Ask a student to join you in the demonstration so he or she can model the thinking process for the rest of the class.

- Consider asking students to record in a learning log why it's important to consider multiple perspectives before forming an opinion about either Cortéz or the Aztecs. Then ask them to share their thinking with a partner.

- For students who have not yet studied writer's voice in your language arts or English program, you may need to explain the term and provide a few examples before asking them to analyze different perspectives of a historical figure or event. Consider letting some students participate orally.

Part D

For either final summarization task, students may jot down their thoughts in a bulleted list and defend their points orally, if that will ease the anxiety of students who get bogged down in the writing portion of the task.

Responding to the Needs of Advanced Students

For advanced students, we may need to create some extensions. Here are some suggestions:

Allow advanced students to work together to complete each of the small-group activities. Ask them to identify parallels between Cortéz and the Aztecs and other eras and events of human history, such as the conquests of Alexander the Great, the rise of the Roman Empire, and the expansions of the United States and United Kingdom and their territories. Students can compare what they've learned about Cortéz to the United States government's actions during the "Manifest Destiny" phase of the country's westward expansion or how any country known for imperialism took control of a new region and affected its inhabitants.

Once they have identified these connections, ask students to record at least two lessons about humanity or government that we should have learned from such experiences, but did not. For example, as of this writing, there is debate among diplomats as to whether Iraq, a country being torn apart by sectarian violence, should be divided into three smaller countries. Would dividing it into three separate countries help or hinder the conflicts within the country? Is this the best option for a country dealing with such deadly insurgencies? How does a country rebuild itself after civil war?

Because a culture is defined as the behaviors and traits associated with a particular population, we could ask students to consider the criteria we might use to determine a culture's superiority over others. This has applications to understanding and appreciating different neighborhoods within our own communities—or futuristic societies. For example, consider the *Star Trek* television and movie series, which raised ethical issues worth students' attention, such as whether we should interfere with a society that is in the process of destroying itself, whether technology always represents an advancement, and what we lose when we blend cultures without maintaining their distinctive identities. We could even ask students to debate the value of having one dominant language or many languages—which is a wiser move for a region? a planet?

Advanced and gifted students also can search for other primary and secondary sources that would provide alternative perspectives about Cortéz and the Aztecs. They may pursue Cortéz or the Aztecs in greater depth, such as with a satellite study, also known as an "orbital" study (Hollas 2005), in which students provide the class with a more thorough view of either Cortéz or the Aztecs based on personal research that goes beyond the basic curriculum.

Students who are interested in technology and gaming can compare a particular video or role-playing game and the relationship Cortéz forged with the Aztecs.

Students can also direct media coverage of the events under discussion, including those of past eras that did not have media technology at the time. They can create a newspaper or photojournalism essay, including editorials, for example, about the Aztecs. Or, perhaps they'd be interested in developing a make-believe blog site featuring short commentaries, feedback from readers, photos, and links to other Internet resources about the Aztecs and Cortéz.

Finally, consider letting a group of students stage a trial in which the world court considers Cortéz's treatment of the Aztec people. Ask students to portray the event in two parts: one in which Cortéz successfully defends his actions and the second where the evidence clearly points to his guilt. To prepare students for this activity, show them how to investigate the prosecution of recent historical figures charged with crimes against humanity, such as Saddam Hussein and Slobodan Milosevic. Help them understand the nature of criminal proceedings, including how the prosecution and defense might present different interpretations of the same evidence and events.

Be aware: These are all good activities for students identified as gifted or advanced learners, but such students aren't necessarily prepared to work independently or wisely just because they are capable of complex thinking. We can't just say to students, "Go do this. Have fun. Explore, and I'll return to your classmates while you're off on your intellectual adventure."

With all *students, make the implicit explicit, the invisible visible.*

Just as with students who are on grade level or who are struggling to learn, we must scaffold instruction and coach advanced learners through the essential steps. Some teachers make the mistake of setting the bar unusually high for these students and assuming all of them can reach it without assistance. This is not true—children are children, all with different life experiences and proclivities, even in the gifted world.

With each of the activities for advanced students suggested above, be prepared to break them into smaller tasks and subsets of skills and teach these concepts to students, or at least significantly facilitate their own learning of them. Make the invisible visible, just as you'd do with any other student. Teach advanced students specific aspects of this project, such as how to analyze websites and other sources for accuracy and balanced perspectives. Teach them how to portray a person who believes differently than we do, and help them know when they have enough information to draw a conclusion.

In addition, realize that some of these activities might appeal to students who haven't been identified as advanced or gifted. We need to ask ourselves tough questions about our practices and challenge our initial assumptions about students. Do we offer struggling and regular education students the same experiences? How about a portion of them? Are we being elitist? Are we careful not to create, as one friend put it to me recently, the "bluebirds and larvae reading groups of yesteryear"?

We differentiate for students who need differentiation. Occasionally, a student may not be identified as advanced, but may demonstrate sophisticated understanding and skill in a particular unit of study. It's appropriate in these instances to invite the student to be a part of the advanced curriculum; it would be a disservice not to do so.

The goal is being attentive to students' readiness levels, not limiting them to labels—high, low, or something in between. Are we open to changing our perceptions of students' readiness levels in the course of our lessons? For students who are not identified as gifted, do we still provide them with a range of appealing choices and push them to stretch their thinking and skill development? Dynamic learning experiences are not the exclusive domain of the gifted and advanced. However, most students identified as gifted or advanced have demonstrated clear and consistent evidence of unusually well developed knowledge, skills, or proclivities. These are habits of performance, not accidental flukes of behavior. Advanced students are normally comfortable when tackling complexities or working within their skill range, high as it is. Students who are not yet ready to operate at such advanced levels are easily frustrated when asked to do so. In a well-intentioned effort to provide gifted experiences for the regular education student, we can cause undue stress and even dysfunction.

Most students are not happy when they are placed in situations that provide repeated evidence of their incompetence. They feel hurt, anxious, and even angry. When they experience success, they are more likely to participate and take risks with their learning. This is true of all students.

We need to establish informal and formal means for monitoring the appropriate level of challenge for students. We respond to what our students present to us, and these behaviors can change from week to week. This is another call for frequent formative assessments throughout our lessons to guide instruction and provide feedback.

While monitoring and responding, we can takes steps to make sure our classroom culture emphasizes acceleration without making less advanced students feel inferior. If we regularly adjust the pacing and manner of instructional delivery and share Gardner's multiple intelligences theory as well as descriptions of learning styles with students, we can create a culture that accepts differences, including the rate and complexity of learning.

Let me make this appeal as well: I've been teaching gifted students along with regular education students for almost twenty-five years. Once in a while, when I've been absent due to illness or inservice training, colleagues helped cover my classes when no substitute teacher was available. Upon returning to my classroom, I discovered that many of these colleagues were very anxious about teaching the sections of my schedule dedicated to whole classes of advanced learners. In addition, some of these folks made comments to students such as: "Well, that's not 'honors-level thinking.'" "I thought gifted students were supposed to be smart" (said when a student did something typically foolish, as most fourteen-year-olds will occasionally do). "How did you get in such an advanced class with behavior like that?" Sadly, even some of my colleagues who teach advanced, honors, or gifted classes regularly make the same remarks.

I'm not sure why these teachers feel the need to constantly parade labels in front of gifted students. Is it a way to keep them in their place? Are teachers nervous that these students will somehow outsmart them? Actually, that *should* be happening in all of our classes, if we're doing our job right.

Before I really knew and understood gifted and advanced students from the teacher's point of view, I suppose I felt the same way—a little anxious that they would see my faults and limitations. There were two perspectives, however, that changed my thinking.

First, teachers who feel threatened by advanced learners may think the instructor is supposed to be a water tank of knowledge from which students drink daily. The teacher dispenses a finite amount of knowledge over time, and when that's all gone, there is nothing left. They assume that if students surpass the capacity of the teacher to feed their thirst, the balance of power will shift.

The trick to getting over this anxiety is remembering that we're not supposed to know it all. We teach students how to learn for themselves. While we may open many doors for students, we don't open all of them.

Second, we must remember that we are dealing with young adolescents, no matter what their IQ scores might indicate. Sometimes they will forget their pencils; this doesn't mean they're not intellectually gifted, only that they're twelve years old. Sometimes they will be moody and argue with everything we say; this doesn't mean they're not gifted, only that they're fourteen years old. Sometimes they will act impulsively and shoplift a bottle of Gatorade, ride in the back of a friend's pickup truck at fifty miles per hour, or skip a class; this doesn't mean they're not gifted, only that they're sixteen years old. The moment we realize that gifted and advanced students still need a mentor with common sense and someone to listen to their concerns, share a laugh, and forgive their digressions, we relax as a teacher; *this* is something we can offer our students, regardless of our own proficiencies.

Differentiating in Advanced Placement and International Baccalaureate Classes

Teachers of Advanced Placement (AP), International Baccalaureate (IB), and similar courses initially may feel frustrated by suggestions to differentiate, because the nature of their courses is strictly prescribed by protocols from the organization that accredits their program. Their courses are very structured and often presented with clear imperatives for quick pacing through intense curriculum. There appears to be little time to formatively assess students, let alone adjust instruction in light of what those assessments indicate.

The question these teachers should ask, however, is whether or not it is acceptable to not differentiate when it is needed. If a student is not successful with the existing one-size-fits-all pacing and manner of teaching, then what does a caring and highly effective teacher do? Do we plow ahead in the program without offering assistance or alternative strategies to the student? No. This would be callous and ineffective.

The bottom line for all such advanced programs is that high-caliber students should learn the material well. The program creators are supportive of teachers who make curriculum relevant to the students they serve. Teachers in advanced programs such as these have been differentiating instruction for students as they can—for those who struggle and for those who need something even more advanced—for years. Programs that are structured and advanced don't preclude differentiated practices. Students are still students in need of strategic, responsive teaching. If we find a way to help a struggling student regain his or her footing, then we're doing what we're supposed to do. If we occasionally deviate from the prescribed path in order to maximize students' learning in these programs, we're still achieving the program's goal; there's no dilution of content or skills.

Finding the time to truly teach something well as opposed to merely presenting it will always be a problem for differentiating teachers, especially those who teach advanced courses with heavily loaded curriculum. Taking a step back, however, and looking at the larger goals and whether or not the alternative of doing nothing would be acceptable provides ample justification for us to differentiate whenever we can without fearing that we are diminishing the integrity of the advanced program.

Three Questions to Guide Our Brainstorming of Lesson Modifications

In looking back at the suggested modifications for all of these students, you may wonder how I generated this list of differentiated activities. Three major questions guided my work:

1. What misunderstandings are likely to occur during the unit, and how can I prevent them?

2. Given the composition of my class, how can I meet the needs of all students and ensure that they benefit from the learning experiences?

3. Do these alternatives help me and my students focus on the lesson's objectives? Put another way: Am I holding students accountable for learning the same information and skills, though they may scale those heights from different directions?

Changing Our Lesson Plans As We Respond to Students

Even well-designed lessons will need tweaking. Recognizing this, it's okay to deviate from the script once in a while, especially when something new inspires us or we're responding to the unforeseen needs of our students. These impromptu decisions often lead to some of our most effective teaching moments.

Let's identify some scenarios that could occur when teaching the lesson about Cortéz and the Aztecs and how we might handle the situation.

Students laugh at the invader and don't take the staged event seriously.

- Apologize to the students for not foreseeing this interruption and putting a stop to it, but remain in character: concerned, serious, and a little unnerved.

- If the laughter gets out of hand, let students see the "behind-the-scenes" work of the lesson. Tell them that you designed the experience as an opening "hook" to create interest in the lesson instead of resorting to more mundane activities such as reading a chapter in the textbook and answering questions. Remind students that you could quickly switch to a slower, less compelling activity if the laughing doesn't stop. Anyone who continues to detract from the experience can be asked to leave (moving to a colleague's classroom to complete an assignment for ten minutes while the rest of the class finishes the simulation). You will have a serious discussion with this student later.

- Tell the volunteer to stop, and ask the disruptive students for their names and the names of their parents. This usually makes students nervous and quiet.

- Stand next to the laughing students and glare at them sternly. Give these students a sharp desist command while looking concerned about the intruder.

Students take the invader too seriously and become upset.

- Break character and ask the invader to take a bow and introduce himself or herself to the class. Give the volunteer a small acting award—half a sheet of paper on which you've quickly scribbled "Academy Award for Acting" or a sculpture quickly made from aluminum foil in the shape of a statue of "Oscar" from the Academy Awards.

- Discuss the metacognitive aspects of the lesson. Remind students that simulation is a powerful way to learn information, and tell them that you wanted to move the content into long-term memory by making it vivid. If the activity continues to bother students, apologize sincerely.

- Consider giving some students roles in the drama so they will feel more in control. This is particularly effective for overly excited or talkative students.

Students can't come up with any ideas for what our communities will look like in fifty years.

- Ask students to identify another person, real or imagined, with a strong personality and predict the changes that person might prompt in a community. For example, what new rules might a favorite cartoon character, movie villain, sports star, musician, or literary character make?

- Ask students to consider how the world changed because colonists created the United States of America. Or, ask them to consider what the world would look like today if the United States never existed.

Students have no idea how a conqueror might benefit a conquered people.

- If students know about Marco Polo, ask them to consider how Polo shared ideas and products discovered during his travels with different societies along the trade routes.

- Discuss the ways that a technologically advanced culture might affect a less advanced culture.

- Ask students to consider how the formation of the United States affected the original inhabitants of North America. Although the westward expansion created conflicts, particularly with Mexico and Native American tribes, it led to some benefits as well. What are they?

The video is too long. Students' attention wanders.

- Break the video into shorter segments of no more than ten to twelve minutes each. Ask students to process what they've just seen orally or in writing before moving to the next segment.

- Stop after the descriptions of the major effects of the invasion and ask students to record their thinking on graphic organizers. Provide a few moments for them to talk with a partner prior to completing the task, if that will help. Do not allow them to record their notes while watching the video—that will dilute the learning experience.

- Use a think-aloud (self-talk) activity to reinforce the proper way to watch a movie, looking for the five major ways Cortéz's invasion affected the Aztecs.

Students can't identify an impact that Cortéz had on the Aztecs.

- Stop and rewind the video and view a particular segment with the class a second time. Ask a student who understands the task to watch the video and describe her thinking aloud as she watches.

- Stop the video at strategic moments and ask guiding questions that lead students to their own discovery of the impact. Once you've walked through one of the segments, give students a chance to reflect on their own. Let them share their thinking with a partner before continuing with the rest of the video.

Students identify a negative impact as a positive result.

- Ask the students to explain their opinion. As they reexplain, they may realize the error of their thinking. Paraphrase the thinking back to them, "So what you're saying is…" and see if they agree or disagree.

- Ask whether or not the generalization would apply to similar situations, something more immediately relevant to their own lives. Choose an example that would definitely reveal the incorrectness of their conclusion.

- Ask students to redefine what is meant by *positive* and *negative*.

- Ask students to provide evidence of their claim. Ask other students to support or refute the conclusion with clear evidence, then ask the first students to offer a solid rebuttal to their classmates or to revise their statement.

One or more of the five sources that students are supposed to analyze are too difficult for some to read or interpret.

- Pair struggling readers with fluent readers and allow the fluent readers to read aloud.

- Put the text on a cassette tape or DVD and let struggling readers listen to it. Read the text aloud as students follow along silently.

- Purposely choose primary source documents with lower readability levels.

- Provide a typed or printed version of a text that was originally written in cursive handwriting. Break the text into shorter sections and ask students to analyze each section individually.

- Provide an overview and/or flowchart of the main ideas in the text before asking struggling students to read it. This creates a mental road map of what they can expect while reading the material, and they can refer to the navigational tools as they read.

- Give struggling students more time to complete the task. Or, don't require them to refer to as much of the text as other students.

- Encourage struggling students to identify the overt, vivid examples while fluent readers identify more subtle messages. This doesn't mean you will never encourage struggling readers to look for subtleties in literature, but it does mean you will tier the experience according to their readiness level.

Students still do not understand why they should look at multiple sources or consider diverse perspectives before forming opinions.

- Identify some common features of students' lives that could be misinterpreted by someone who does not understand their culture. Examples include:

  - Why does everyone go into their homes in the evening—are we afraid of the darkness? Does something emerge at night that we don't want to encounter?

  - We don't usually worry about the deciduous trees that lose their leaves during the autumn months. But a visitor from another planet or a country that does not experience similar seasonal changes might misinterpret this process as environmental decay. Science fiction writer Charles Sheffield offers a take on this shift in perspective in his wonderful short story "That Strain Again" (1996).

  - We yell profanity.

  - We hold up a cigarette lighter at the end of a rock concert.

  - We clap our hands together in applause when we are pleased by another person's performance.

  - We diaper human babies but not animals.

  - We pay for expensive clothes, electronics, cars, and vacations when we say we care about poor people who can't afford such luxuries. Why don't we give our extra money to them?

  - We shake each other's hands in greeting.

  - We put animals in cages at the zoo.

  - We burn our skin while sunbathing.

- Brainstorm historical events that could be interpreted in more than one way. Ask students to identify the effects of different interpretations, such as the United States bombing of Japan during World War II.

Students' portrayal of Cortéz or the Aztecs in the writer's voice activity is inaccurate.

- Ask students to explain their rationale for choosing the tone in their writing. Absent specific evidence, ask them to redo the assignment, paying careful attention to voice.

Steps to Take While Designing and Implementing the Learning Experiences   **57**

- Provide examples of correct and incorrect reflections. Provide at least three different strategies to evoke a specific voice in writing, including word choice, sentence structures, point of view, topics mentioned, figurative language, pacing/rhythm, tone/attitude, and other stylistic devices. For more on writer's voice, consult the numerous resources available on 6 + 1 Trait Writing. The 6 + 1 Trait Writing approach creates an accessible framework and language for teaching writing and revising across the grade levels. Suggested authors include Vicki Spandel (2004) and Ruth Culham (2003). The website www.nwrel.org is also an excellent resource.

Students do not write a satisfactory summary at the end of the lesson.

- Identify the elements of an effective summary and ask students to evaluate their work in light of the following criteria:

  - Does my summary convey the information accurately?

  - Is my summary too narrow or too broad? Does it convey all of the important elements?

  - Would someone who used this summary understand the full impact of Cortéz's invasion of the Aztecs?

  - Did my summary include personal opinions?

  - Did I use my own words and writing style?

- Ask students to write a practice summary on a familiar topic, get feedback from you or another teacher, then revise the summary of Cortéz.

Students don't finish a task on time.

- Let students finish the rest of the assignment at home.

- Reduce the number of tasks assigned.

- Let students complete the task orally.

- Let students provide bulleted summaries rather than respond in complete sentences.

- Provide time later in the class period, the school day, or the school week so students will get another chance to finish whatever assignments they have not yet completed.

- Divide the tasks among the group members and ask them to compile their work as if they were completing a jigsaw puzzle.

Reminders When Reviewing Our Differentiated Lesson

As you may recall, differentiating teachers incorporate several additional steps in their lesson design and implementation:

- Run a mental tape of each step in the lesson sequence to make sure that the process makes sense for your diverse group of students and will help the lesson run smoothly.

- Review your plans with a colleague.

- Obtain/create materials needed for the lesson.

- Conduct the lesson.

- Adjust formative and summative assessments and objectives as necessary based on observations and data collected while teaching the lessons.

Take the time to run that mental tape every time you teach. Review your plans at least twice a year with someone who is supportive of your efforts to differentiate. Lesson design is one of the most subjective aspects of instruction. We need an objective perspective from someone who didn't write the lessons to find the missed opportunities and trouble spots.

Finally, don't forget the organic nature of lesson design, objectives, and assessments. Anything can be adjusted at any time for any reason; nothing is set in stone. I consider teachers with messy lesson-plan books—the ones with cross-outs, sticky notes, erasures, notes written diagonally in the margins, and arrows moving from one square to another—exemplary. These marks suggest that the teachers are responding to the students they have before them each day, adjusting and readjusting. They are maximizing instruction, not trying to protect the pristine nature of their planning.

Messy lesson plans can be positive things!

I worry about teachers who plan their lessons moment by moment for the next two, three, and even four weeks, then stick to those lessons no matter what happens. The homework they record for three Thursdays from today is, by golly, the homework they assign that third Thursday from now. Their prescience is amazing! Additionally, I worry about the principal who asks for specific lesson plans for the following week to be placed in the office before teachers leave for the weekend. That same administrator expects to see the lesson as described whenever he walks into a class at any point that following week.

Both of these examples can lead to ineffective teaching. Principals who engage in such micromanagement are more interested in compliance and control than student learning. Unaltered lesson plans provide a false sense that all is well.

Before someone misquotes me, please understand what I just said. I'm concerned about teachers who don't adapt. Planning our lessons in advance is wonderful—I do it myself. Sticking to the plan when it's not working is reckless, however. In my own practice, I usually prepare lessons weeks in advance, but I tinker with them every night and sometimes in my mind while in the shower or on the way to school. My planner is full of corrections based on new inspirations or insights I've gleaned from students or colleagues. This approach enables me to meet the needs of a classroom with diverse learners.

And yes, occasionally, my lesson plans are pristinely recorded without a single erasure, cross-out, arrow, or sticky note. This is because I recorded the lessons in the plan book only *after* teaching them. I just hadn't found time to transfer the summary I wrote on the Pizza Hut napkin while dining with my family the previous weekend.

I also recognize that in some schools faculties are engaged in Critical Friends groups, action research groups, or professional learning communities, which expect lesson plans to be submitted for administrative or collegial review. This is an excellent practice I heartily endorse. I would have paid someone to do this for me during my first years of teaching. Come to think of it, I'd welcome the same chance today. In such situations, teachers are treated as professionals. They not only are able to change their lesson plans, but are invited to do so if it would make their lessons more effective.

In addition, if a teacher has been struggling to provide effective instruction, an administrator *should* ask for his or her lesson plans in advance. This is supportive, not punitive. And, because principals need a fairly intimate view of what's happening in their schools, *all* teachers, not just new teachers, should submit a fully developed lesson plan in writing at least once a year as well as a monthly list of the general topics to be taught in their classrooms. Quick classroom walk-throughs by principals may or may not reveal this information. As the faculty's leader and the prime liaison to the community, the principal must be informed.

However, veteran teachers with a proven record of successful differentiation should not be asked to submit lessons for weekly review. Such requirements greatly increase a teacher's workload in an already overloaded job with something that does not significantly improve the quality of teaching or students' achievement. Anything that we can do to ease the demands on teachers so they can spend time on effective instruction and assessment, we should do.

* * *

At this point in the development of a differentiated lesson from scratch (remember the empty computer screen with a blinking cursor?), let's remind ourselves of the whole sequence we've followed.

1. Identify your essential understandings, questions, benchmarks, objectives, skills, standards, and/or learner outcomes.

2. Identify those students who have special needs, and start thinking about how you will adapt your instruction to ensure that they can learn and achieve.

3. Design formative and summative assessments.

4. Design and deliver preassessments based on summative assessments and identified objectives.

5. Adjust assessments and objectives based on further thinking discovered while designing the assessments.

6. Design the learning experiences for students based on the information gathered from those preassessments; your knowledge of your students; and your expertise with the curriculum, cognitive theory, and students at this stage of human development.

7. Run a mental tape of each step in the lesson sequence to make sure that the process makes sense for your diverse group of students and will help the lesson run smoothly.

8. Review your plans with a colleague.

9. Obtain/create materials needed for the lesson.

10. Conduct the lesson.

11. Adjust formative and summative assessments and objectives as necessary based on observations and data collected while teaching the lessons.

As you look over this formal outline of how to plan for differentiation, remember, too, that differentiation is often done informally—on the fly. Because we're conscientious educators, we provide extra examples for students if they need it, we offer a different metaphor to explain something to students who are confused, and we don't make advanced learners slog through curriculum they have already mastered. Whether we plan formally or respond flexibly without prior planning, our mind-set is the critical factor. Do we actively pursue assessment of and with students as they learn? Are we willing to adjust instruction as a result of what we discover? Do we have the large repertoire of responses necessary to be able to adjust instruction accordingly?

Look for informal ways to differentiate as well.

If you recall from the beginning of the chapter where I described the design sequence, there are two additional steps to take after the planning process. Let's examine them briefly here.

Steps to Take *After* Providing the Learning Experiences

With Students, Evaluate the Lesson's Success

If time allows (and if it doesn't, find a way to make it happen anyway at least once a month), get reflective. Take a few moments and ask yourself,

- What worked, and what didn't?

- If something worked, how do I know? What evidence do I have that my students learned the content and skills I intended to convey?

- If the lesson didn't work, what will I need to change the next time I teach? And what will I need to do with my students tomorrow to help them achieve?

- Did I meet the varied learning needs of my students? If so, how?

- If I was nervous about one or more elements, how did they turn out?

- What surprised me?

- What do I now know that I wish I had known before I started this lesson or unit? What advice would I give a colleague who might use these materials in the future?

- Which students still need help to learn essential skills?

- Did the sequence of the lesson work? If not, how would I rearrange it?

- How would a highly accomplished teacher improve this lesson?

Engaging in professional self-analysis might seem awkward at first, but it's vital for effective differentiation. Better yet, ask a colleague to listen to your responses. Publicly articulating your rationale makes the ideas real and will encourage you to think about them on a deeper level. You will be more likely to internalize the lessons and put your insights into action if you have to defend your positions with someone else. Try this at least once or twice this year. Choose a colleague who wants to grow professionally as well.

Record Advice About Possible Changes

"Tickler File" Ideas

These are tips and reminders you want to have on hand when you use this lesson again. Place these suggestions in the real or virtual folder in which you store everything associated with this unit of study. Be sure to reference it as you plan next year. Examples from this lesson might include the following:

- Decrease the number of rules the intruder announces.

- Break the video into shorter segments and process each segment individually.

- Turn this into a two-day lesson. There's too much material for a single class period.

- Don't ask students to consider all of the other perspectives. There are some overlapping ideas. Search for more distinctive examples, or simply reduce the number.

- Find more examples that reflect the Aztecs' perspectives.

- Design most of these activities to be used with the entire class (or, conversely, with small groups).

Reflecting on your lessons and recording your insights will improve your future practices. It's important to make time for this process. No matter what you discover while you're teaching the lesson, you will soon forget it and probably repeat mistakes unless you review the impact of your decisions and note it. Teachers continually tell me how much these reflections expand their skills and increase their effectiveness in the classroom.

This ends the step-by-step approach of differentiation design. Of course, our lessons may not go according to plan, so we will want to have a collection of differentiation "tools of the trade" handy for such occasions. The next chapter includes some recommended techniques.

Chapter 3

Helpful Structures and Strategies for the Differentiated Class

Differentiation can happen both formally as we design our lessons according to learning models and informally as we adjust our lessons in the course of teaching them, such as when walking by a student's desk, noting a mistake, and deciding to stop and reteach the concept. To be flexible and employ the most effective techniques at the most strategic times, we need a large repertoire of responses ready to apply at any moment.

This section provides more than a dozen effective differentiation practices and structures that will help you refine your instruction. These practices are commonly used by teachers who are successful with diverse groups of students. I have presented them here as an initial description of the practice or structure, but the hope is that you will pursue further understanding of these ideas by experimenting with them in your classroom, discussing them with colleagues, and reading more about them in the resources recommended later in the book.

The practices and structures fall into two categories: "General Differentiation Approaches" and "Tiering." Both sections include principles and practical tips, but the tiering section also contains strategies aimed at the various learning levels that may be represented within a single classroom.

General Differentiation Approaches

Different, Not More or Less

With differentiation we strive to change the nature of our assignments, not the quantity. If we give bright students double the normal number of assignments, they will start playing dumb to avoid the excess. Instead of asking them to complete thirty math equations while their classmates focus on fifteen, vary the complexity of the problems and their applications. Give these students *different* work, not *more* work.

When designing activities and assignments for your more advanced students, avoid thinking in terms of keeping them busy until the others can catch up. Instead, identify what students already know and help them move beyond their initial understanding, even if this means soaring past what *you* know about the subject or topic. Take a look at the section on compacting the curriculum, page 90, for more information about how to do this.

Try to maintain a roughly equivalent work load for all students, regardless of their readiness levels. By work load, I refer to the time and energy needed to complete the task. As long as these are roughly the same, we haven't changed the work load. For example, some students can balance twelve chemical equations in the same time that other students can balance five. The students have reached different levels of proficiency with chemistry. Both sets of students need fifteen minutes to complete their tasks, but we are not increasing or decreasing the work load by varying the number of tasks. Both sets of students have expended the same time and energy.

Let's consider this from another angle. When we first teach a skill or topic, we generally want to limit the number of required tasks so students can focus on learning the basics. As they gain proficiency, they can work more rapidly when practicing the concepts until they develop an almost automatic response or recall. At this advanced level, we often *want* them to complete more tasks in the same amount of time to demonstrate their increased proficiency. As the process unfolds, we maintain the same work load (time and energy needed) for students despite changing the number of required tasks according to their needs.

Keep in mind that while it may be appropriate to ask students to quicken their pace with some tasks, we don't want to require expediency in all learning situations. For much of the curriculum, knowing how to do something or how to learn more about a topic will suffice. For example, we might teach students to recognize direct and indirect objects in English or weigh rocks and minerals using a balance, but we don't make them race through a dozen related tasks within ten minutes. Understanding, not expediency, is the goal.

As you plan your differentiated lessons, ask yourself: Am I changing the work load or am I changing the nature of the task? Stay focused on changing the nature of the task in most cases. With some students, however, ask yourself: Are my students ready for introductory concept attainment, or are they ready for something more advanced that includes building expediency with the topic? If they are at the initial stage, it may be more prudent to give them fewer tasks that they can successfully complete in a longer time period than ask to them to attempt many tasks quickly, which will merely frustrate them. Aim for a constructive learning experience, not a 100-yard dash.

Adjust Instruction Based on Assessment Results

Some teachers view assessment through a narrow lens—as the test questions or projects that come at the end of a lesson or unit. Such summative results can help us determine students' mastery of standards or learner outcomes, but they represent just a small part of the assessment data teachers can collect and analyze to improve achievement.

Effective assessment involves both gathering data and using it to adjust our practices. We shouldn't spend hours analyzing students' learning styles, interests, personality types, backgrounds, and readiness for learning specific content and skills and then disregard the information, plowing ahead with what we were going to do anyway. What a waste!

In a differentiated classroom we don't separate assessment from instruction. We weave these two essential components of teaching together on the premise that we cannot have good assessment that does not instruct, and we cannot have good instruction that does not assess. Assessment should inform our practices at every turn. Consider two examples of how we can do this on a recurring basis.

In her expository writing, Tamika repeatedly makes general claims without providing supportive evidence. When the teacher notices this pattern in Tamika's latest essay, he designs a quick mini-lesson to show Tamika the difference between writing that incorporates strong argumentation and evidence and writing that offers weak substantiation. After discussing the comparisons in published samples, he reinforces a previous lesson about how to find and report research. Finally, the teacher asks Tamika to analyze the evidence and citations presented in samples of students' work (samples without names and identifications in order to protect students' privacy).

While working with Rafael to create a PowerPoint presentation about the differences between DNA and RNA, the biology teacher notices that Rafael mentions RNA's many roles in protein synthesis in the presentation but does not mention that some types of RNA carry genetic information from a cell's chromosomes to its ribosomes—a point she wants to make sure he and his classmates know. In addition, Rafael writes lengthy text explanations for each PowerPoint slide when the point of the assignment is to write short, bulleted summaries of the major findings. In response, the teacher asks Rafael to review the rules for creating PowerPoint presentations and revise his slides accordingly. Then she asks him to discuss the difference between RNA and DNA and their roles in cell physiology. Finally she asks Rafael to make sure that the information on his slides corresponds with the correct scientific facts.

Realistically, with thirty to thirty-five other students in the classroom, teachers can't assess and adjust their instruction for every student every time it's necessary. Over the course of a week, however, teachers generally can find time for multiple individualized sessions, using alternative structures and activities (see the Football and the Anchor descriptions beginning on page 91) to keep other students engaged.

Because the interaction between assessment and instruction is so crucial, teachers who differentiate try to spend the majority of their time designing and implementing formative assessments—more time, in fact, than they spend designing summative assessments. Sure, those summative assessments are important—they create direction for all we do—but formative assessments have the most impact on students' learning.

In addition, while formative assessments lead to students' mastery, they do not demonstrate final mastery, nor are they meant to do so. Instead, formative assessments provide useful feedback to students and teachers about their ongoing progress. As a result, formative assessments can have a much greater impact on student achievement. This is so important that over the years I've reinforced my intentions with formative assessment by reviewing my lesson plans week by week and circling every formative assessment listed. If I found only one or two examples in a given week, I added others.

Although we typically prepare and record formative assessments in our lesson plans, we also can informally assess students through classroom conversations, observations, and spur-of-the-moment products that we ask students to create. As a result, formative assessments don't have to be large and complex. They are often straightforward and directly related to what we're teaching. Here are some examples of formative assessment prompts we can record in our lesson plans as we design differentiated lessons or that might occur to us in the spur of the moment as we teach:

- Identify at least five steps you need to take in order to solve math problems like these.

- How would you help a friend keep the differences between amphibians and reptiles clear in his or her mind?

- Write a paragraph of three to five lines that uses a demonstrative pronoun in each sentence and circle each example.

- Play the F-sharp scale.

- In a quick paragraph, describe the impact of the Lusitania's sinking.

- Create a web or outline that captures what we've learned today about . . .

- Solve these four math problems.

- What three factors led to the government's decision to . . .

- Draw a symbol that best portrays this book's character as you now understand him (her), and write a brief explanation as to why you chose the symbol you did.

- Record your answer to this question on your dry-erase board and hold it above your head for me to see.

- Prepare a rough draft of the letter you're going to write.

- What is your definition of . . .

- Who had a more pivotal role in this historical situation, _____ or _____, and why do you believe as you do?

Notice that some of these quick, formative assessments can work as summative assessments as well; this is exactly as it should be. Great formative assessments are often small pieces of summative assessments examined separately. If formative assessments are a subset of the final assessment, we can use them to evaluate students' progression toward the lesson's goals and adjust instruction accordingly. If formative assessments are not related to the summative assessment, they won't provide the data we need to chart the journey ahead.

"Exit cards" are often used for formative assessments. These brief exercises or reflections give us quick insights about how well students understood our lessons. For example, before we transition to another section or task, we can ask students to punctuate five sentences correctly based on their new understanding of comma placement in divided quotations. Or, we might ask students to briefly describe the correct way to determine velocity or to identify at least three errors in a sample science lab report. We can provide additional differentiation through the prompts we use for exit cards. Depending on the students' readiness levels, we might ask some to identify examples of assonance and consonance in poetry but ask others to create poetry that uses assonance and consonance for a desired effect. Exit cards should be short and easy to review, making it efficient to assess students quickly and make appropriate instructional decisions.

When do we formatively assess students? Daily, if possible, and every fifteen to twenty minutes, ideally. We can't always take the time to do this with a formal product, of course, but we can also include in our formative assessments a general "reading" of students via their actions and facial expressions while we're teaching: Are students responding to questions we pose with substantive answers or less so? Are they able to get started on a task successfully or are they floundering? Are their eyes glazing over or are they attentive? Are students actively looking for excuses to leave the classroom on unnecessary errands (a sign that students are not experiencing enough competence to warrant continued involvement in something that reminds them of how much they don't understand) or do they not want to miss anything?

We have to take the temperature of the room frequently to be successful. For instance, in the course of teaching students to make metric conversions within the metric system, such as converting meters into decimeters, centimeters, and millimeters; grams into kilograms; and milliliters into cubic centimeters, my first formative assessment in the lesson would come after teaching students the metric terms such as *milli*, *centi*, *deci*, and *kilo*. This could be a quick vocabulary assessment in the form of a matching test, quickly drawn numbers on dry-erase boards, a number of fingers held up for the number of place values we move the decimal point, oral responses to individual questions, or something done by each student up at the board. If students didn't know the terms well, I'd go back and reteach the terms. If they passed this formative assessment, I'd move on.

Soon after teaching students how to make simple conversions within the metric system, I'd give them four or five additional conversions to do on their own. I'd look over their responses to see if they have the basic idea. Students' careless errors in this second formative assessment wouldn't prevent me from moving on to the next topic I wanted to teach but would remind me to provide additional practice later. If students made errors that indicated true lack of understanding, however, I'd have to decide whether to move on. In some cases, moving on to the next level of challenge or topic would help students overcome their confusion with an earlier level or topic—the next one providing contextual meaning. In other cases, I would need to stop and reteach those conversion processes.

In this short sequence, I've suggested two formative assessments, each one directing my instruction. I may or may not record these assessments as steps to take in my lesson plan, but I keep searching for ways to use them and adjust instruction based on the data they provide.

For sources that provide more information about formative assessments, see the Recommended Resources.

Modify Options: Content, Process, Product, Affect, and Learning Environment

We can differentiate instruction in many ways, but the methods tend to fall within these major categories, first popularized by Dr. Carol Ann

Tomlinson at the University of Virginia and described in *Differentiation in Practice* (Tomlinson and Strickland 2005):

- *Content:* Our legally mandated curriculum, including all the skills and content knowledge students are supposed to learn

- *Process:* The many ways in which our students learn the curriculum

- *Product:* How students prove that they've learned the content

- *Affect:* The socio-emotional factors that influence learning
    We might need to adjust learning experiences for students to feel safe and invited. Examples include building positive conflict resolution skills among quarreling students, posting exemplary work samples from students who don't typically get noticed, and spending extra time listening to students who seem depressed or upset.

- *Learning Environment:* The classroom configurations that provide the best opportunities for students to learn
    Here we consider factors such as whether special-needs students work in self-contained or regular classrooms; homogeneous or heterogeneous ability groups; single-sex or coed classrooms; adaptive technology and other equipment that can reduce distractions for some students; class periods interrupted by the lunch schedule; and any other structures that might affect a student's success.

Are any of these factors negotiable with students? Would we allow a student to say, "I don't want to learn this, but I want to learn that," or "I don't want to learn it this way, but I want to learn it this way," or "I don't want to take your test, but I want to demonstrate mastery this other way"? It depends.

If the issue concerns our legally mandated curriculum, then what students learn is probably nonnegotiable. When we teach fractions, for example, students must learn about numerators; denominators; improper fractions; mixed numbers; adding, subtracting, multiplying, and dividing fractions; and reducing to lowest terms. If we adjust the content by removing or adding standards or learner outcomes for an entire grading period, we have to declare that we're using an adjusted curriculum, and that's best avoided because of conflicts with local, state, and federal mandates. We might adjust a single lesson to meet the specific needs of students and resume the regular pacing later. We might adjust how we deliver the content while focusing on the same curriculum as well. We can do some adjusting here and there, but we still must rally around the same standards as identified by society as important in this discipline to teach to this age-group.

The techniques we use with students to teach specific content and skills are negotiable unless the lesson is literally about those techniques, which would most commonly happen in teacher preparation institutions only. For example, if we're teaching students how to write a proper introduction to a research paper, we can use different techniques, some more independent of, and some more dependent upon, the teacher. It doesn't really matter which strategies we use or which ones students prefer as long as they learn how to write good introductions.

Students who understand their learning styles can guide us as well. If a student tells us that the flash cards we assigned to help him learn his vocabulary words don't really help him, we should allow him to suggest alternative ways to learn the vocabulary. Insisting that he use the flash cards anyway—something ineffective—would be punitive, and we want to be instructive instead. One of the best ways to help students with diverse learning styles is to not limit them to our imaginations. We can't get so attached to our one method of learning that we are blind to something more effective.

The products students use to provide evidence of understanding can be negotiable as well. It shouldn't matter how students demonstrate their mastery of a topic or skill, unless the focus of our instruction is that specific product. For example, if we're teaching students about the rivalry between Sparta and Athens in ancient Greece, we can assess their understanding through multiple-choice questions, matching games, true/false identifications, fill-in-the-blank exercises, short answer and essay questions, artistic or musical representations, oral reports, creation of a website dedicated to the conflict, one-on-one conversations, and so on. If we're teaching students how to do a PowerPoint presentation, on the other hand, students will have to create a PowerPoint presentation and share it with the class; there are not alternative formats. In this case, we can differentiate *how* we teach students to create these presentations, including adjusting the pacing of our lessons, but the final product will be the same.

Models of Instruction

Many teachers follow Madeline Hunter's direct instruction model (1993; 1994). It's a logical and well-loved approach that can be part of a differentiated classroom. It is ineffective, however, if it becomes the *only* model we use. Teachers who successfully meet the needs of diverse students become adept at mixing and matching multiple models of instruction. I have summarized the most common models below so you will have a frame of reference for your own exploration. The Recommended Resources provides sources for more information about these models.

Direct Instruction

- State objectives and standards for the day.

- Provide an anticipatory set or "hook."

- Teach, including experiences with reviewing previously learned material/homework, input, modeling, and checking for understanding.

- Provide guided practice with feedback.

- Reteach (as needed).

- Review both during and at the end of the lesson.

- Closure (summarization).

- Assign independent practice.

Dimensions of Learning

Designed by Robert Marzano (1992), this model asks teachers to plan their lessons according to five different dimensions.

- Positive Attitudes and Perceptions About Learning

- Acquiring and Integrating Knowledge

- Extending and Refining Knowledge

- Using Knowledge Meaningfully

- Productive Habits of Mind

One-third Model

This is Robert Lynn Canady and Michael Rettig's (1996) method of dividing lessons into instructional sections.

- One-third presentation of content

- One-third application of knowledge and skills learned

- One-third synthesis of the information

Concept Attainment Model

This is a constructivist approach in which

- The teacher presents examples of a formula, concept, or idea being used, and students work with the examples, noting attributes or criteria of the formula, concept, or idea.

- The teacher asks students to define the formula, concept, or idea being learned.

- The teacher critiques more examples of the topic in light of this new thinking.

- Through different activities, students practice and apply their understanding of the concept.

- Students are evaluated through additional applications.

4MAT System

This model appeals to students' different learning styles. According to Dr. Bernice McCarthy (2007), there are four types of learners. Each type represents a particular way in which students learn best. If a teacher provides instruction in the preferred approach, students will learn more.

- *Type 1 Learners* These students respond well to experiences in which they can think reflectively, pondering the *why* of the situation. They seek connections and are good observers.

- *Type 2 Learners* These students respond well to viewing and listening to the facts and concepts expressed by experts. They want to analyze things and know the *what* of the situation.

- *Type 3 Learners* These students prefer to learn by doing. They like to explore and analyze how things work. They seek relevance.

- *Type 4 Learners* These students prefer to explore the *what-if* questions. They like trial and error and making discoveries on their own.

For lesson plans, assessments, and tools for identifying these four learning styles, visit McCarthy's website, www.aboutlearning.com.

* * *

Additional models of instruction and theories of learning that successful differentiating teachers use include Meyers-Briggs (2007) personality types, Anthony Gregorc's (1999–2007) scale and teaching model, Howard Gardner's (1983) multiple intelligences theory, and Rita Dunn's (2007) learning style inventories. Try to find time to learn one of these new models and others each year that you teach. The single greatest tool you have as a teacher is your knowledge about how the mind learns. Get up to speed on the latest thinking by exploring models and theories of learning.

Flexible Grouping

Some students learn best through individual study, some learn best from small-group interactions, and some through whole-class instruction. There are many arrangements teachers can create within each of these major categories. However, for all the variety, many teachers use only one or two of these groupings in their classrooms. That's unfortunate because it means they may not be maximizing instruction for all students.

The "ebb and flow" of instruction (Tomlinson 2003)—moving from larger groups to smaller groups to independent study, and back again—is an important part of differentiated instruction. As we plan our lessons, it's helpful to ask some candid questions about our use of flexible groupings.

- Is this the only way to organize students for learning?

- Where in the lesson could I create opportunities for students to work in small groups?

- Would this part of the lesson be more effective as an independent activity?

- Why do I have the whole class involved in the same activity at this point in the lesson?

- Will I be able to meet the needs of all students with this grouping?

- I've been using a lot of [*insert type of grouping here—whole-class, small-group, or independent*] work lately. Which type of grouping should I add to the mix?

As we differentiate, we should become familiar with a range of flexible groupings, including:

- Whole class or half class

- Teams

- Small groups led by students

- Partners and triads

- Individual study

- One-on-one mentoring with an adult

- Temporary pull-out groups to teach specific mini-lessons

- Anchor activities to which students return after working in small groups

- Learning centers or learning stations through which students rotate in small groups or individually. Although commonly used in primary grades, learning centers can be appropriate for middle and high school students as well.

  For example, learning stations in a math class might include activities that require students to use physical manipulatives as they explore a concept while another station might include activities that require students to work with the same concepts using only symbolic and abstract terms. In a foreign language class, learning centers might include headphones, CDs, and compact disc players that students can use to practice hearing and pronouncing words and phrases. Other stations could ask students to read and interpret written text emphasizing regular and irregular verbs.

Flexible groupings enable us to move students fluidly through our lessons. Whole-class instruction might be fine for a lab demonstration, but if we want students to practice an experiment, we'd choose one of the smaller groupings, such as working in pairs or triads. If some students don't feel comfortable talking in front of the class, we give them opportunities to work with one or two partners until they become more confident. If we have to teach different subtopics concurrently to a whole class, centers and anchor activities may be the way to go. To engage students, we may occasionally form competitive teams. If we feel some students are relying too much on the work of others in their small groups, it may be time for some independent work so we can monitor each student's individual progress towards a learning goal.

Teachers are always looking for ways to manage groupings of students. One management technique found in many differentiated classrooms is "Clock Partners."

Students can stagnate if they always work with the same peers. To encourage a variety of collaborations without creating burdensome record-keeping, ask students to identify clock partners. To set these up, let students move around the room and identify classmates who would be willing to partner with them. To correspond with the twelve numerals on a clock, they will need to find twelve peers. They can't be too choosey—they need a lot of partners.

Partners agree to work together at a particular time. For example, if Steve is Miguel's 4:00 partner, Miguel writes Steve's name in the 4:00 slot on the clock face he's created, and Steve writes Miguel's name in his 4:00 slot on the clock face he's created. (See Figure 3.1 for an example of a sample clock partner form. A reproducible page of this form is included in the

FIGURE 3.1 Sample Clock Partner Form

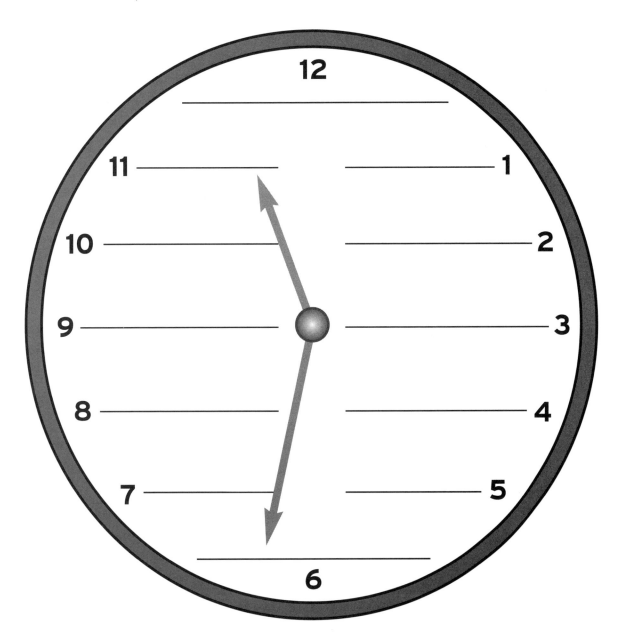

Appendix.) Continue this process until all time slots are filled. After the time sheets are completed, collect them and review them to make sure every slot is taken by an appropriate partner, then return them to students and ask them to keep these clocks in the front portion of their notebooks or binders for quick reference.

Another format that may be more familiar to students is an appointment calendar, such as they might find on a PDA or in computer scheduling software. Figure 3.2 shows a sample of one.

At the appropriate time, ask students to refer to their clocks or appointment calendars and consult with the identified partners. You might say, "Please work with your 7:00 partners and prove the theorem on page seventy-one. Then you and your partner should join another partner team and compare your approaches—were they successful or not? What would you change?"

Some teachers rightfully caution colleagues who use clock partners or similar systems for choosing partners because these practices can hurt the feelings of students who are not chosen right away or at all. This is a good point, and if this strategy bothers you or if you know the relationships in a particular class are less than friendly choose a more random selection process instead. Place students' names on popsicle sticks and pull names out of a can two at a time to create partner teams. Or, simply form partners based on your knowledge of who might work well together and

FIGURE 3.2 Sample Appointment Calendar

7:00 A.M.: _____

8:00 A.M.: _____

9:00 A.M.: _____

10:00 A.M.: _____

11:00 A.M.: _____

12:00 P.M.: _____

1:00 P.M.: _____

2:00 P.M.: _____

3:00 P.M.: _____

4:00 P.M.: _____

5:00 P.M.: _____

6:00 P.M.: _____

announce the partnerships to the class. If you use clock partners, ask students to select different classmates each time until they have exhausted all the possible combinations.

If the activity is one in which it's okay for friends to work with friends, such as when playing a review game or working on something of mutual interest, it might be okay for students to choose their own partners, but it may still leave a few students feeling isolated, or at the very least, merely tolerated because the teacher is commanding the partnering.

Remember that if you choose the partners, you'll be the focus of students' appeals to change them from time to time. This is normal. Decide in advance how you will handle these appeals: No changes for one week, then you'll consider it? No changes, period? Deciding each case on its merits? Whatever you do, it's worth spending time to teach students how to work with someone with whom they disagree or don't like before they begin to work with partners. That's a skill critical to students' emotional growth and academic success.

Play with the flexible groupings and see how students perform in different settings. Keep in mind that a favorite arrangement one week may not work the following week but may work again later in the year. Try to roll with it. Differentiation helps us become more adaptive. Our openness to new experiences can inspire students to take similar risks, and vice versa.

Collaboration with Students

Teaching is not a one-way street. Be open to the fluid nature of learning. Students are our partners in education; they are not just the clients or the passive recipients of our knowledge. If you're struggling to find an effective way to reach students, consider asking them for ideas. Notebook reflections and informal report cards in which we ask them to evaluate our performance are just some of the ways we can gather feedback. No one should expect us to know how to differentiate instruction and assessment for all students every day. We'll get closer to the ideal when we realize that good solutions often come from the collective wisdom of both teachers and students. In differentiated classrooms, teachers and students collaborate to deliver instruction.

Personal Agendas

Some students become lost in the general lesson plan. The classroom experience is too distracting or the students are not organized enough to keep up with the group. They need specific steps to follow.

Providing an individual agenda on a piece of paper these students keep at their desks can serve as a checklist to keep them focused and show their progress (Hollas 2006). Keep the personal agenda as close as possible to the goals for the rest of the class, but you may want to add details for some students to break the lesson into manageable chunks and/or help them remember steps.

When designing a personal agenda, try to use a computer so you can keep track of both long-term and short-term skills that need reinforcement. Some students might need regular written reminders to take out a pencil, place homework in the upper right-hand corner of the desk for the teacher to check, and complete the warm-up work on the SMART Board located at the front of the classroom. Other agenda items might pertain to a specific lesson.

Figure 3.3 shows a sample personal agenda for a student. At first glance, this agenda seems to involve a great deal of preparation. Keep in mind that you would only do this for students who really need it. Some students who drift off task can be refocused with a brief verbal or physical signal (saying their names, standing next to them, using their names in

FIGURE 3.3 Sample Personal Agenda

Daily Tasks:

1. _____ Place last night's homework at the top right corner of the desk.

2. _____ Record the warm-up activity from the front chalkboard in your learning log.

3. _____ Respond to the warm-up activity.

4. _____ Listen to the teacher explain the lesson's agenda for the day.

5. _____ Record the assignment from the Homework Wall in your notebook.

Specific to Today's Lesson:

6. _____ Get a copy of the graphic organizer from the teacher and put your name and date at the top.

7. _____ Fill in the example while the teacher explains it to the class.

8. _____ Read both sides of the graphic organizer so you know what you are looking for.

9. _____ Watch the video and fill in the graphic organizer during the breaks.

10. _____ Complete the closing activity for the video.

11. _____ Ask Ms. Green to sign your assignment notebook.

12. _____ Go to math class, but first pick up math book in locker.

the lesson) or by giving them something with which to fidget while listening, such as a stress ball.

You probably won't need to maintain the personal agenda for the entire school year. You may use it to guide a few students for a few weeks at a time.

The extra initial time you spend preparing these agendas should save you time in the long run by reducing behavior and other classroom management problems. You won't need to reteach students who weren't focused the first time. You won't have students acting out because they're frustrated; personal agendas provide physical proof of their accomplishments. For these reasons, agendas can be worth the hassle.

Tiering

A Slightly Different Definition

Tiering generally refers to the ways teachers adjust instruction and assessment according to the learner's readiness level (the capacity to handle different levels of challenge in an assignment), interests, and/or learner profile.

I'm not sold on this brief definition because it seems to reflect more lateral than vertical adjustments. Of the three variations, only readiness suggests a hierarchy of skills. In contrast, one student's interest in basketball isn't a higher tier than another student's interest in swimming. One student's intrapersonal intelligence isn't higher or lower than another student's proclivity for spatial thinking. Adjusting instruction to accommodate students' interests and learner profiles represents a horizontal strategy, not a layered, vertical approach implied in the word *tiering*.

So I'm going to use the common term but combine it with Carol Ann Tomlinson's explanation of ratcheting (1999)—adjusting the complexity of tasks and experiences to redesign instruction and assessments based on students' readiness to learn.

Tomlinson's Equalizer

Tomlinson encourages us to consider more gradations, such as designing activities that will move students towards greater independence and juggle multiple variables. These tiers form a continuum of skills reflected in Tomlinson's Equalizer (Figure 3.4), a popular tool found in many books and websites, a number of which are included in the Recommended Resources section of this book.

FIGURE 3.4 Tomlinson's Equalizer

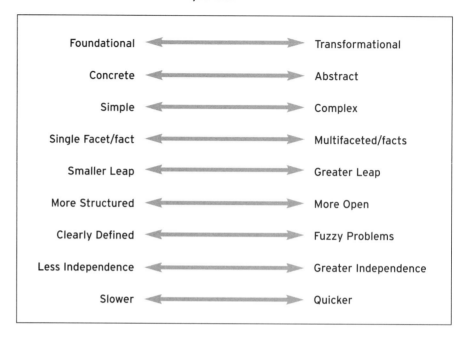

We can use the equalizer to evaluate our assignments as well as our students. For example, Becca is a quiet student who's ready for more challenge. She's been completing the regular assignments for weeks without complaint, but her teacher has noticed the sophisticated connections that Becca has made between her personal reading (she always has a novel at hand!) and other subject disciplines and current events. Using the Equalizer, the teacher realizes that Becca is ready for open-ended assignments and experiences that incorporate more than one variable and enable her to make larger leaps in thinking.

This time, looking through the lens of the lesson plan, the teacher decides to adjust an upcoming assignment based on the Equalizer. Instead of asking Becca to define science terms, the teacher encourages her to read through several suggested experiment proposals and determine which will yield the most useful data for scientists and decision-makers.

Later, the teacher asks Becca to extend the scientific terms—*quantitative* and *qualitative analysis*—to poetry. What would constitute quantitative analysis of poetry, the teacher asks, and what would constitute qualitative analysis of poetry?

Becca's quantitative analysis might include the number of allusions to cytology (study of the cell) in the selected poem, the uses of figurative language, the rhyming pattern, meter, number of lines per stanza, and a comparison of these statistics with the poet's previous and subsequent works. The teacher also asks her to notice any change in these numbers as the poet aged and to try to attribute the changes.

For qualitative analysis, Becca might evaluate the poem using the general criteria for a specific type of poetry, such as focusing on the characteristics of a sonnet, narrative poem, haiku, or a poem with specific meter. Becca examines whether or not the poem follows the model, is a hybrid of some sort, or something that breaks the mold entirely. She looks for the specific effect the poet sought for his intended audience as she listens to the poet read the piece aloud, and she identifies strategies the poet employs to create that effect. She might categorize the poetic devices used and consider whether they helped or distracted the reader. Did the poet use the correct science, or did he fudge it in some places to fit the needs of the poem? Once these extensions are explored, the teacher brings Becca back towards the focus of the general science lesson and asks her to conduct quantitative and qualitative analyses of complex data sets obtained from an experiment conducted in class.

The Equalizer provided the catalyst for reflection the teacher needed to meet Becca's needs.

Gradations of Mastery

The Equalizer gives us a great starting point for our differentiated lesson design. The levels on the continuum suggest a journey from early, introductory understanding of a topic to more sophisticated reasoning. As we design differentiated lessons, we need to carefully consider this progression.

Imagine a lesson in which we are teaching students to infer. We can use concrete and vivid examples of inference, and we can use symbolic and abstract connections.

Here's a quick lesson at the introductory level.

A student walks into the classroom while wearing a heavy coat, pretending to shiver, and saying, "Brrrr!" For fun, the teacher places some crushed ice or fake snow on the student's shoulders. Next the teacher asks students to draw a conclusion (make an inference) about the weather outside based on the data presented by their classmate's portrayal and their own background knowledge.

Here's a more abstract experience with inference.

As students read Remarque's *All Quiet on the Western Front*, the teacher asks them to gather citations from the text to help them determine what the author was inferring about government propaganda during World War I.

The first example is rather basic, easily experienced by a quick observation and comparison with prior knowledge. The second example requires more thought. There is no vivid portrayal to observe, and students have probably not had much experience with this type of commentary on government propaganda.

Teachers who are experienced with differentiation will identify both of these levels—introductory and sophisticated, as well as the gradations in between—then skillfully guide students toward full mastery. Let's look at these levels in relation to several topics.

Surface Area of Three-Dimensional Solids

Introductory

Sophisticated

1. Determine the surface area of a cube.

2. Determine the surface area of a rectangular prism (a rectangular box).

3. Determine the amount of wrapping paper needed to cover a rectangular box. Don't forget to overlap the paper along the edges so you can tape the corners neatly.

4. Determine how many cans of paint you'll need to buy in order to paint a three-story house with the given dimensions, if one can of paint will cover forty-six square feet, and you are not to paint the windows, doorways, or external air vents.

Vocabulary Terms

Introductory

Sophisticated

1. Define the vocabulary terms.

2. Compare the vocabulary terms.

3. Use the vocabulary terms correctly in conversation or writing.

4. Use the vocabulary terms strategically to obtain a particular result.

Sumer and the Fertile Crescent

Introductory

Sophisticated

1. Identify the characteristics of Ancient Sumer.

2. Explore the connections between religion and government in Sumer.

3. Explain the rise and fall of city-states in Mesopotamia.

4. Trace modern structures/ideas back to their roots in the birthplace of civilization, the Fertile Crescent.

Cellular Biology

Introductory

Sophisticated

1. Identify the parts of a cell.

2. Explain the systems within a cell and what functions they perform.

3. Explain how a cell is part of a larger system of cells that form a tissue.

4. Demonstrate how a cell replicates itself.

5. Identify what can go wrong in mitosis.

6. List what we know about how cells learn to specialize in the body.

7. Explain how knowledge of cells helps us understand other physiology.

Multiplying and Dividing Fractions and Decimals

Introductory

Sophisticated

1. Multiply fractions.

2. Multiply mixed numbers.

3. Multiply mixed numbers and whole numbers.

4. Critique the solutions of five students' work as they multiply mixed numbers.

5. Multiply mixed numbers and decimals.

6. Divide fractions.

7. Divide mixed numbers.

8. Divide mixed numbers and whole numbers.

9. Given similar problems completed by anonymous students, identify any errors they've made and how you would reteach them how to do the problems correctly.

There are many ways to raise and lower the complexity of an assignment for students. I've sorted through these strategies throughout my career and created my own list of strategies that help me address students' diverse needs. I staple this list into my lesson-plan book every year and frequently reference it. Some of the ideas were inspired by Grant Wiggins, Carol Tomlinson, Susan Winebrenner, and others who have written about differentiated instruction and assessment, and some of the ideas are my own, but all of them work in multiple subjects and grade levels. A version of this list originally appeared in my book, *Fair Isn't Always Equal: Assessment and Grading in the Differentiated Classroom* (2006). I have updated it and included additional examples. For each one, ask students to

- *Manipulate information, don't just echo it.* "Once you understand the motivations and viewpoints of the two historical figures, consider how each one would respond to the three ethical issues provided."

- *Extend the concept to other subjects and topics.* "How does this idea apply to the expansion of the United States railroads during the nineteenth century?" Or, "How is this sort of interaction portrayed in the Kingdom Protista?"

- *Integrate more than one subject or skill.* "Identify the limiting factors of the human habitat of Chicago during the industrial revolution. How would we determine its carrying capacity?"

- *Increase the number of variables that must be considered; incorporate more facets.* "Change the lab procedure so the three given potential sources of contamination are no longer a factor." Or, "Now that you've designed a more energy efficient type of human transportation vehicle that operates on renewable fuels, design a similar human transportation vehicle that can be operated in a deep-sea research colony. Be sure to account for salinity, depth/pressure, the three-dimensional biologics (animals) that live there, air supply and proper mixture, water-tight construction, and easy egress and regress."

- *Demonstrate higher-level thinking as indicated in ascending levels, such as in Bloom's Taxonomy, Williams's Taxonomy, or something else.* "On each of the six faces of a posterboard cube you create, interact with our topic via the following prompts: Describe it. Compare it. Associate it. Analyze it. Apply it. Argue for it or against it."

- *Use or apply content/skills in new or different situations.* "As part of our service project, we need to fill this large rectangular sandbox in the playground with sand. How many cubic meters of sand do we need to purchase by Saturday in order to fill the box?"

- *Make choices among several substantive ones.* "Identify the three possible ways the character could resolve the dangerous situation before him, then weigh each one against your own code of ethics. Which one would you choose if you were in the situation, and why?"

- *Work with advanced or primary resources.* "Using the latest schematics of the Space Shuttle flight deck and real interviews with professionals at Jet Propulsion Laboratories in California, prepare a report that ....." Or, "Here is the raw data for immigration to New York City from 1920 to 1930. What can we conclude from it?" Or, "Create a robotic device that performs the following five tasks in sequence."

- *Add an unexpected element to the process or product.* "What could prevent meiosis from creating four haploid nuclei (gametes) from a single haploid cell?" Or, "How might the world be different if President Truman had lost the election?"

- *Reframe a topic under a new theme.* "Rewrite the scene from the point of view of the antagonist." Or, "Reconsider the United States' involvement in war in terms of insect behavior." Or, "Retell *Goldilocks and the Three Bears* so that it becomes a cautionary tale about McCarthyism."

- *Work independently.* "Please do this on your own, without the assistance of parents, teachers, or classmates."

- *Share the backstory to a topic.* "Why are so many factions interested in controlling the West Bank and Gaza Strip?" Or, "What was going on in the author's life when he wrote this, and did it have an effect on his observations?"

- *Identify the misconceptions.* "What myths does this student unknowingly promote in his essay on the President of the United States?" Or, "Does the news reporter's description accurately portray the event? Explain your reasoning."

- *Identify the bias or prejudice.* "Examine the presentation of this news story on three different television networks. Identify each network's slant for the story and note what was included or not included in order to create such a slant."

- *Negotiate the evaluative criteria.* "Examine these four samples of exemplary [labs/essays/projects/speeches/performances] and identify at least five common characteristics that demonstrate quality. Afterward, identify features of this project that would provide evidence of quality. Be prepared to defend your choices."

- *Deal with ambiguity and multiple meanings or steps.* "Explain both sides of the argument compellingly." Or, "Argue for the opposing side of the debate, regardless of your personal views." Or, "Identify the multiple connotations of *fire* in the poem."

- *Use content/skills in real-world applications.* "Compose and send a business letter using proper business-letter format to a real company of your choosing. You can request more information or replacement parts or compliment and thank the company for a good product." Or, "Maintain accurate bookkeeping for your theater production as you purchase supplies, pay for advertising, sell tickets, and provide refreshments and programs for patrons."

- *Analyze the action or object.* "Break the process down into six important steps." Or, "What are the essential ingredients of this policy?"

- *Debate the merits of something taken for granted or commonly accepted by others.* "Should we expose all children to chicken pox so they will get chicken pox when they are young?" Or, "Is this book and the values it promotes appropriate reading for all students at this age?"

- *Synthesize two or more seemingly unrelated concepts or objects.* "How are grammar conventions like music?"

- *Critique something, using a set of standards.* "Evaluate the student's choral performance against the criteria we identified for excellence."

- *Consider and report on the ethical ramifications of a policy or act.* "Do the potential benefits of genetic engineering of humans outweigh the possible risks?" Or, "Is the federal government ever justified in restricting an individual's rights to protect other citizens?"

- *Work with abstract concepts and models.* "Explain how logarithmic functions are the inverse of exponential functions." Or, "Identify how the artist uses balance, movement, and unity to engage the viewer."

- *Respond to open-ended situations.* "Brainstorm possible resolutions to the gang conflict in our town." Or, "What are the current roles of men and women in society, and how will they change in the next twenty-five years?" Or, "Identify three or more ways to solve the problem, not just one."

- *Increase expediency with a skill.* "Identify the errors in the following text, which is longer than you edited last time." Or, "Do twenty problems of this type, now that you know how to do this." Or, "Identify the most expedient way to tabulate the data."

- *Identify big picture patterns or connections.* "What is the larger category into which this fits?" Or, "What conclusions can you draw from this information?" Or, "How will knowing this make the character able to respond successfully to the conflict?"

- *Defend their work.* "What is the evidence for your claim?" Or, "Would others draw the same conclusions as you have done here?" Or, "Provide a flowchart of your thinking." Or, "Identify potential arguments against your stance and respond to them compellingly."

As you work with your students and the curriculum, consider the continuum of skills that will lead from an introductory level of understanding and performance to an advanced level. The creative challenge is providing different paths for students to move from novice to expert. Tomlinson's Equalizer and the previous suggestions for adjusting complexity can spark our thinking.

Respectful Tasks

If the focus of a lesson is teaching students how to write a conclusion to an essay or report, we should ensure that all students are learning to write conclusions. This may seem obvious, but many teachers think they are differentiating when they give students alternative tasks that have little connection to a lesson's objectives. For example, some students may not be ready to fully analyze a period of history that we're teaching, so we ask them to create an inviting travel brochure about the era to use as an advertisement for future time-travelers. What does this teach them about historical analysis? Not much.

Instead of providing an unrelated assignment, we could tier the lesson with respectful tasks. For students who are struggling to learn, we might break off the chunks they *can* do and progressively add complexity. In a lesson about historical analysis, students at the introductory level of understanding may be able to tackle only one aspect of the period or the culture under consideration—perhaps scientific progress or religion. For students in the middle range, we could ask them to consider two or three ideas but limit the amount of evidence required to substantiate a conclusion. Or, we might prime their minds by asking them to first analyze something much closer to the modern age. For advanced students, we might ask them to analyze multiple aspects of the historical period along different themes, require primary resource evidence to substantiate their claims, or use the identified themes to compare the historical period to modern times.

The point of respectful tasks is to never drift far from standards of excellence and to provide meaningful (developmentally appropriate) experiences for all students. Consider how this purpose plays out in the following scenarios.

In a math class, a student is struggling to learn how to divide decimals, so the teacher

- Asks him to critique the methods used by several anonymous students, some of whom followed the correct approach and some of whom didn't. The student uses a list of evaluative criteria mutually agreed upon by the teacher and student. *(example of a respectful task)*

- Asks him to make an attractive bulletin board for the classroom that defines all the math terms used when dividing decimals. *(example of an unrelated task)*

In an English class, a student already understands irony before the lesson starts, so the teacher

- Asks her to identify two examples of irony in modern usage or to rewrite the last scene of a short story to reflect irony. *(example of a respectful task)*

- Asks her to write an acrostic poem about irony (I stands for _____, R stands for _____, and so on). *(example of an unrelated task)*

By the way, if we accept the premise that all assignments should be developmentally appropriate, then the grades we obtain from students' work will remain accurate and fair. If we grade an activity that has little to do with the focus of our lesson, the task becomes a means to baby-sit the student while the rest of the class catches up, and any grade earned is useless to both the teacher and the student.

Compacting the Curriculum

If some students demonstrate advanced readiness early in the unit, we shouldn't waste their time focusing on skills and content they already understand. Instead, we try to shorten the process, making sure they've mastered the basic curriculum and double-checking their knowledge of more subtle points. Then we provide extensions that enable the students to explore important details in greater depth or breadth, consider a theme from a unique angle, or develop projects that include teaching someone else what they've learned.

For example, if a group of students already knows how to set up one type of media presentation software on the computer, we can teach them about other multimedia tools. If we don't know how to use these tools ourselves, we could direct students to related resources or experts in the field. Afterward, the students can present their findings to the class.

We have very little time with students, and there's so much for them to learn. Forcing them to plow old ground means they can't discover new territory. The heart of differentiation is recognizing that each student may follow a different path to knowledge. Compacting the curriculum is an effective way to unleash their potential.

The Football and the Anchor: Teaching a Variety of Levels at the Same Time

Many of us see teaching as a linear, step-by-step process, but this approach limits our imagination and our effectiveness. Because students usually are at different levels of readiness for learning, we need to design a sequence of tasks that will let each of them progress, no matter where they started.

Two structural sequences that enable teachers to reach a diverse group of students at the same time are the "football" and the "anchor." Okay, I know this sounds cheesy, but I'm going to write it anyway: Let's tackle the football first.

The Football Structure

The football metaphor comes from the way we think about the lesson's sequence: a narrow, whole-class experience in the beginning, a wider expansion of the topic as multiple groups learn at their own pace or in their own ways, then a renarrowing as we gather again to process what we've learned. In short, a football, as shown in Figure 3.5. (Figure 3.5 also appears as a blank form in the Appendix.)

FIGURE 3.5 The Football Structure

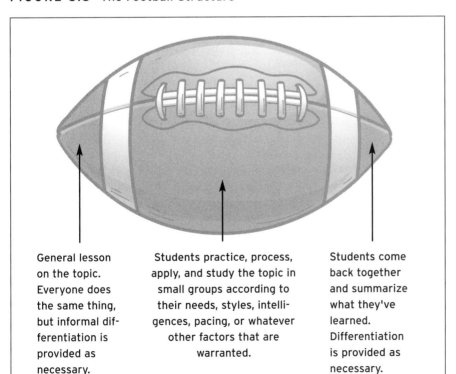

General lesson on the topic. Everyone does the same thing, but informal differentiation is provided as necessary.

Students practice, process, apply, and study the topic in small groups according to their needs, styles, intelligences, pacing, or whatever other factors that are warranted.

Students come back together and summarize what they've learned. Differentiation is provided as necessary.

In this three-part sequence, we first teach a general lesson to the whole class for ten to fifteen minutes. Although we might differentiate here and there as warranted—such as providing a second example to study, adjusting the pacing, using preferential seating, or allowing the use of calculators for those who need them—most of the students will be engaged in the same activity. We're providing a predominantly whole-class learning experience.

After the general lesson, we divide the class into groups according to readiness, interest, or learning profile and let them process the concepts at their own pace or in their own way. This wider, middle section of the lesson lasts for fifteen to thirty minutes. While students work in small groups or independently, we circulate throughout the room, clarifying directions, providing feedback, and answering questions.

We can vary this middle section extensively to meet the needs of students. We might have two groups interacting with the topic of the first section at different levels or nine groups focusing on a different aspect of Gardner's theory of multiple intelligences.

Here's an example of this topic expansion from my own classroom: Students were studying World War II in one of my colleague's history classes, and I was teaching literature about the Holocaust in my English class. In addition to discussing how authors make their novels historically authentic, we were exploring the way characters evolve through conflict in narratives. I divided my students into groups according to their reading levels.

Some students used excerpts from *The Diary of a Young Girl* (Frank 1993), while others used excerpts from *Good Night, Mr. Tom* (Magorian 1982), *The Devil's Arithmetic* (Yolen 1988) and *Lisa's War* (Matas 1989). Each of these books has different levels of complexity, including Yiddish (Yolen), dialect (Magorian), intense content (Frank, Yolen, Magorian), and use of conflict to advance the story and characters (all four), as well as varying reading levels. Students focused on the same universal elements—character evolution and historical authenticity.

Once students have explored the initial content and skills through small-group exercises and individual tasks, they are ready to come together as a whole group and process what they've learned. This is the final portion of the football instructional metaphor. This processing can take the form of a summarization, a question-and-answer session, a quick assessment, or some other specific activity that engages students and enables them to debrief with each other. This phase usually takes about ten to fifteen minutes.

Figure 3.6 includes a 3–2–1 activity that I used during the previously mentioned study of authenticity in literature. A 3–2–1 activity is a summarization task in which the student is asked to respond (in writing, drawing, or speaking) to three prompts.

One of the great aspects of the football sequence is that all students can contribute to the final conversation in substantive ways. In the previous

FIGURE 3.6 3-2-1 Activity for Group Processing of
Narrative Authenticity

3 Working with a partner, identify three techniques authors use to create authenticity in their historical narratives.

2 Working with the same partner, write a quick scene that takes place in any other historical era and uses two or more techniques authors use to create historical authenticity. You will need to understand the period of history well to complete this task.

1 Working independently, identify one piece of advice you would give writers trying to make their narratives more authentic to the period.

Remember that you may need to adjust the complexity of the summarization prompts to meet the needs of students from time to time.

example, everyone can comment on how authors create authenticity in a novel. Everyone could observe how characters change and grow as a result of conflict in a story. Everyone had the right tools (although they might not have been the same as those used by their peers) to achieve the same learning outcome.

The Anchor Structure

When I was first learning to differentiate, I realized I had students who were performing below, on, and above grade level, yet I only had one class period a day to teach all of them. If I concentrated on each level or need in linear sequence, I couldn't address all the issues by the end of the week, much less by the end of the class period, nor could I complete the curriculum I was supposed to teach. I also didn't want to give up my breakfast, lunch, after-school time, or planning period to reteach lessons for students who didn't learn concepts and skills the first time, nor did I want to require additional commitments from students. I didn't mind occasional overtime, but not every day.

The question was, how could I be in two or more places working with two or more groups of students at the same time? In other words, how could I teach a variety of students concurrently, all within the same class period? It was while trying to solve this problem that a colleague mentioned anchor activities to me, and I was hooked, though admittedly I took this technique in a different direction.

Many books, videos, and presentations about differentiation explain anchor activities as tasks that teachers use to maintain momentum in the classroom, such as when they ask students to complete puzzles or read ahead to the next chapter while waiting for classmates to finish a test. To

FIGURE 3.7 Visual Anchor Metaphor for Classroom Planning

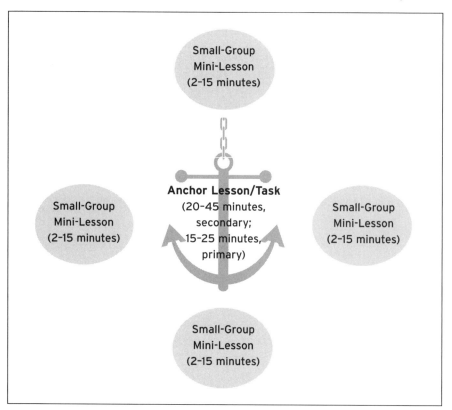

me, such tasks are better described with the metaphor of a sponge—activities that soak up time. By contrast, an anchor activity to me should be more substantive and truly root the lesson, not just keep students occupied. Figure 3.7 shows the visual metaphor for classroom planning. (A blank version is included in the Appendix.)

In an anchor-lesson structure, the teacher assigns a task for the entire class to complete autonomously. As students work individually, the teacher is free to gather small groups of students for mini-lessons based on their needs. After the mini-lesson, she sends the students back to the main activity and rotates to another small group. In a band or orchestra class, for example, the teacher can pull several students to one side to practice their fingering for a complex set of measures. With another set of students she can provide feedback on yesterday's performance, and with yet another group she can discuss techniques they have been working on after school with private instructors. While the teacher assists each group in rotation, the rest of the band members tune their instruments, warm up, or practice their individual portions of the upcoming concert.

The mini-lessons a teacher designs can be as simple and informal as stopping by a student's desk to explain how to use a semicolon or as complex and formal as teaching students how to determine the weight that structures will bear in a physics experiment. The focus of the mini-lesson doesn't have to be related to the day's topic. Teachers also can use this time to reinforce separate skills and concepts that will improve students' learning overall.

Three components must be in place for the anchor lesson to succeed. First, students must know how to work independently. During anchor lessons, the teacher will focus on small groups and individual students and shouldn't be interrupted except for emergencies. If students become confused while working on the anchor activity, they should try to solve the problem before asking the teacher. To help students develop autonomy, the teacher can remind them of the steps to take before asking for assistance. Here are some suggestions.

Suggested Steps for Students to Take When the Teacher Is Not Available

- Draw a picture of what you think it says or asks.

- Move on to the next portion, then come back to the trouble spot later. Something may trigger an idea.

- Reread the directions or previous sections to see if you missed or misinterpreted something.

- Read the directions and/or your response aloud.

- Find a successful example and study how it was done.

- Ask a classmate: "Ask Me," "Graduate Assistant," and "Technoid" (see sidebar on page 96 for helpful tips).

- Define difficult vocabulary.

- Try to explain the topic or idea to someone else.

It's helpful to create a "Ten Things to Do *Before* Asking the Teacher" poster for the room. Ask students for suggestions so there are plenty of options as well as student ownership.

The second essential component of a successful anchor lesson is making sure students understand the tasks involved. Teachers inexperienced with this approach often design large and complex tasks, and students aren't clear about the expectations, what the final product should look like, what resources to use, or how to break the objectives into basic steps. When students don't understand the anchor activity, the teacher will function like a fire chief—calling out directions, interrupting the job at hand, and stamping out new blazes.

The third essential component is having multiple parts of the anchor activity. Reading a personal-choice novel for forty-five minutes might

"**Ask Me**" refers to primary-grade situations in which a designated student "expert" on a topic wears a visor or baseball cap with *Ask Me* written on the visor. The teacher has already determined that these students have advanced skills or competencies with the task and recommends that their classmates consult them. ASCD's video series "At Work in the Differentiated Classroom" (2001) shows clear examples of these visors in action.

"**Graduate Assistant**" is the older-student version of the Ask Me visor. The teacher places triangular tent cards with the words *Graduate Assistant* at designated students' desks. Again, the teacher identifies these students and encourages others to seek their advice when stuck. Because most students will not be familiar with the concept of a graduate assistant, the teacher explains how they function in a university setting.

"**Technoid**" refers to those students with computer or technology expertise who would be helpful if anyone has a problem with either.

If you use one of the first two examples as one of your support structures for anchor activities,

make sure to rotate every student into this position at least once during the year. If a struggling student hasn't had a turn, find a way to teach him or her the basic material for an upcoming lesson at least a day or two ahead, then assign the student the role of Ask Me or Graduate Assistant expert on the day of the lesson. Also make sure to "seed the classroom" with questions and needs, and make sure you are unavailable to assist students. Seeding the classroom means that we set up challenges for the larger class with which they will definitely need assistance from a knowledgeable student, and we ask some students to seek assistance from the expert.

It may be necessary to subtly manipulate the circumstances to give chronically underachieving students an opportunity to shine. It's important for their classmates to consider them competent, and it's crucial that all students have at least one chance during the year to feel the self-confidence and moderate euphoria that come from being perceived as an expert.

work for some students on some days, but it won't work every time. Design the anchor activity to include several steps that involve different cognitive and physical skills, if possible. The task(s) should be substantive and directly related to the curriculum. Here are sample anchor activities from different disciplines.

History Read pages 45–52 about the Industrial Revolution. Identify the five principles that the labor unions representing employees in the meat-packing industry were fighting for. Next, design a flag that includes symbols for each idea. Finally, write a short paragraph describing the flag's symbols.

Math Identify the number of faces, edges, and vertices for each of the following three-dimensional shapes: cube, rectangular prism, rectangular pyramid, triangular pyramid, triangular prism, pentagonal pyramid, pentagonal prism, and cylinder. Next, draw the patterns for each shape on paper. Finally, use the two-dimensional patterns to build the three-dimensional shapes.

Language arts Draw and label a plot profile of the novel, making sure to include markers for the setting, rising action, conflicts, climax, and resolution of the major conflict. Next, draw a second plot profile, but this time pretend that a character from another book is inserted into the story at the midpoint and has a major influence on the outcome of the story. Draw the new changes into the plot profile and explain in writing how the story might change based on this new character's appearance.

Here are some other tips for creating and using anchor activities.

- Require students to turn in a product by the end of the allotted time. This increases their sense of urgency and accountability.

- Start small. Begin with just two groups—assigning half of the class to each—then work toward developing multiple groups.

- Occasionally videotape students as they work on anchor activities independently. Use the video to demonstrate proper and improper behavior. Showing a ten- to fifteen-minute segment should be enough to make an impression.

- Use task cards, which are large index cards or 8½-by-11-inch sheets of paper with the directions and examples listed clearly for students to follow. Task cards can be particularly helpful when you have students at multiple readiness levels working in groups as part of their differentiated learning experience.

- Use a "fish bowl" simulation to show the class how a small group of students should work on a related task while other students complete the main assignment. In this scenario, students observe the actors as they would view fish in an aquarium and use score sheets to evaluate the performance based on previously discussed criteria.

- Train students to disengage from one activity and move into another one successfully. It's worth taking the time to practice moving in and out of small groups or moving from high-energy activities back to quieter individual activities and speeding up the rearrangement of desks or tables or cleaning up one's work space. Practice these transitions multiple times, helping students become familiar with your expectations and expedient in their execution.

Scaffold Instruction

Scaffolding is when we provide direct instruction and support for students as they initially learn a concept or skill, then slowly pull back until students can fly solo. For example, we might ask students to follow a precise guide when they first learn how to write an editorial, but later we'll ask them to play with the format freely, moving pieces around for the best effect. In a foreign language class, we scaffold the instruction initially by asking students to conjugate an irregular verb using a cloze text (students fill in the blanks of sentences with the correct verb tenses) method. Later, students choose their own verb conjugations from a list we provide. And later still, they apply their knowledge during conversations.

When we first use an anchor activity in a differentiated classroom, we need to be very direct about the process we want students to follow, and we carefully sequence the steps. Later we gradually pull away those structures and let students monitor their own behavior and productivity. In the first anchor activity we do, for example, we might ask students to complete five small tasks with very explicit directions, one after the other, without deviation. As students become proficient, we ask them to identify the steps they'd like to take in order to finish the task and get the steps approved before starting. Later, we assign diverse tasks but students must figure out how to do them with minimal advice from the teacher.

Readers may notice the similarities between scaffolding and tiering. There is a difference. Scaffolding is what we do for some students as we tier. It represents another mind-set: Do students have enough direct instruction and support to complete this task, or do they have too much? How can I build their independence with this task by slowly releasing my control of their learning? In *Deeper Reading* (2004), Kelly Gallagher describes three questions that he asks himself before planning a lesson, all of which seem very helpful when thinking about scaffolding (I have added the italics):

- *Without* my assistance, what will my students take from this?

- *With* my assistance, what do I want my students to take from this?

- What can I do to *bridge the gap* between what my students would learn on their own and what I want them to learn? (199)

A part of our teaching mission is to build students' independence. We want them to require less and less direct instruction in order to grow. It's very easy for teachers to make students dependent upon them for learning, but it's a truly successful teacher who has guided students to their own autonomy. Oscar Wilde had it right when he said, "The goal of any teacher is to put himself out of a job."

Chapter 4

Cognitive Science Structures and Tips That Help Us Differentiate

In the past two decades scientists have discovered amazing details about how the adolescent and young adolescent brain works, and this information is crucial to effective differentiated instruction. Without question, the single greatest tool teachers can use is their knowledge of how the human mind learns. Understanding cognitive science gives teachers better ways to reach all students. On some occasions, for instance, we should spend less time thinking about scaffolding, tiering, and flexible groups and more time thinking about how the typical sixteen-year-old (or whatever age you teach) learns. On other occasions, it is through our knowledge of how the brain works that we find effective ways to scaffold, tier, and form flexible groups.

Instead of relying on an occasional inservice training provided by the school or school district, teachers who differentiate effectively keep up with the latest research in cognitive science for students at their grade levels every year. They read widely, attend related conferences or presentations, and discuss what they find with colleagues. The following list includes some of my current favorite resources about how the adolescent mind learns:

How the Brain Learns, David Sousa
The Primal Teen, Barbara Strauch
Brain Matters, Patricia Wolfe
The Adolescent Brain: Reaching for Autonomy, Robert Sylwester
Enriching the Brain, Eric Jensen
Different Brains, Different Learners, Eric Jensen
How to Teach So Students Remember, Marilee Sprenger

To link some of the most important discoveries about brain research to differentiation, let's examine some of the promising practices for teachers in grades five to twelve:

Building Background Knowledge

The human mind commits very little information to long-term memory unless it connects to something already stored there (Sousa 2005; Jensen 2003; Tovani 2001). This means that teachers must consciously tap into students' prior knowledge and if there is no prior knowledge, create it. For example, in which scenario do students learn more?

1. The teacher lets students explore their microscopes: adjusting the light source and rotating the objective lens to see varying degrees of magnification, using monocular or binocular eyepieces, and placing something on a slide with a cover slip and bringing it into focus. Afterwards, students read an article about how microscopes work and answer seven comprehension questions.

2. Students read the article, answer the questions, then investigate the microscope.

In the second scenario, students glance at the text to find the answers to the questions so they can quickly get to the fun part of playing with the microscope. Little information moves to long-term memory because there is no frame of reference. In the first scenario, however, students read the article for deeper meaning because they have some context for the new information and can transfer more of it to long-term memory.

Before examining a famous battle from history, the differentiating teacher provides context and background about what was going on before, during, and after the conflict. Before identifying varied biomes, the differentiating teacher asks students to explore their own habitat. Robert Marzano's *Building Background Knowledge for Academic Achievement* (2004) is an excellent resource for extending these practices.

Priming the Brain and Structuring Information

If we want students to learn concepts and skills solidly, we have to pay close attention to how students first encounter the information. The initial stages of learning should provide clear structures that students can grasp and use to create meaning. Our capacity to retrieve information down the road depends primarily on how we sort and structure concepts and skills in our minds in these early experiences.

For example, if we tell students to memorize random elements in the Periodic Table, we probably won't help them understand or retain the information. A better strategy would be to teach them about the structure of the Periodic Table: The chemical elements are arranged in ascending order according to their atomic number, which refers to the number of protons within the nucleus. The columns of the Periodic Table are further organized into groups, numbering one to eighteen, which have the same number of electrons in the outer shell. The groups are given names according to their commonly held characteristics such as alkali metals, halogens, and noble gases.

Not everything we teach can be structured like this, but more of it can be effectively sequenced than we might think. In English, for example, similes and personification are types of metaphors. When we teach figurative language, we should teach them as subsets of metaphors, not as separate and equal categories. Science and history textbook chapters often focus on a global theme broken down into subcategories or topics. Sometimes the textbooks present information using a compare-and-contrast format, other times in chronological order, and still other times through cause and effect. To make sure all students can comprehend expository texts, we need to teach them how to use these structures.

- We remind some students to read all the titles and subtitles within a chapter to get the gist of the text's structure, then to set up their note taking for the chapter according to those subtitles.

- For other students we create an outline for the chapter's structure that students fill in as they read the text.

- Prior to reading a chapter in the history book, we would help some students identify how the text is presented and how we might structure our notes and thinking. For example, if the transition words and context clues suggest a compare-and-contrast approach of two or more things, we can use T-charts or Venn diagrams to take notes. If the information is presented in chronological order, we can create a time line or flow chart for our note taking.

- To guide their thinking as they read, we encourage some students to create a mind map (a visual representation of the main ideas that incorporates arrows, short phrases, symbols, cartoons, or other illustrations to show one's thinking about a topic).

Just as we might prime a pump to spout water, we provide structure to stimulate students' thinking. Perception is reality for many students, and we have to make sure that we match the substance to the context of their individual experiences.

There are two things that must be communicated to students as we intentionally prime their minds for learning. First, we tell or show them what they will get out of the experience. These are the learning objectives. Teachers often introduce this portion with the phrasing, "As a result of today's lesson, you will know _____ and be able to _____." Second, we tell or show students what they will encounter as they move through the lesson or learning experience. This is the itinerary. Teachers often introduce this portion with the phrasing, "Here are the steps of today's lesson." "Let's take a look at our road map for today." "First, we'll _____, then we'll _____, and finally we'll _____." "Our agenda [or itinerary] includes . . ."

Just before beginning our class's tour of the Smithsonian Institution's Air and Space Museum in Washington, D.C., for example, we'd prime our students' minds for learning. We might say the following:

> As a result of this museum tour, you'll have a much better understanding of flight principles. You'll have clear examples of thrust, propulsion, air pressure, air as mass, air as fluid, Bernoulli's principle, and the curvature of the wing to create lift. As the tour begins, you'll look for evidence of what we've talked about in the classroom this week in the shape of the flying machines on display. Your field trip handout has those specific aspects listed. Next, you'll gather in the IMAX theater to see a film that demonstrates each of these principles. We'll briefly summarize the film's content when it ends. Finally, we'll divide into small groups to interview each of seven pilots who have generously donated their time with us today. They will work with each group to understand the flight principles. Please be prepared to ask at least one question of the pilot regarding these principles. He or she will have supplies available to demonstrate anything you might not yet understand.

For more of the rationale behind priming the mind for learning, check out books on literacy and cognitive science, including Cris Tovani's *I Read It, but I Don't Get It* (Stenhouse, 2000), David Sousa's *How the Brain Learns* (Corwin 2005), and Marilee Sprenger's *How to Teach So Students Remember* (ASCD, 2005).

Primacy-Recency Effect

Many authors and researchers have discussed the Primacy-Recency Effect, but Dr. David Sousa (2005) seems to offer the clearest explanation and applications. Simply put, we remember best what we first experience, and we remember second best what we experience last. This means that the front end and the back end of our lessons are significant learning moments we can't afford to subordinate with clerical or social matters.

When designing our differentiated lessons, we aim to include all the essential ideas or skills in the first ten to fifteen minutes of class and revisit these concepts in the last ten minutes of class through summarization or application. Better yet, we can try to create two or more of these cycles during the class period, which can double or triple the primacy-recency moments. For example, in a fifty-minute class, we could have two cycles that would be twenty to thirty minutes in length. Each cycle would include the beginning, middle, and end points of a lesson, creating two full sequences in effect. In a ninety-minute block class, we might have three cycles, or two longer cycles. It's similar to the oft-referred sequence for lesson design: tell students what you're going to teach them, teach them, and then tell them what you taught them.

The important thing is not to waste the opening moments of class on nonacademic items, including correcting last night's homework, unless it is absolutely impossible to proceed otherwise. Make announcements and attend to other clerical matters in the middle of class. It's just as important not to squander the last minutes of class by cleaning up, organizing, or asking students to start on their homework. The last moments of class are better spent connecting with the major components of the lesson we want students to carry forward.

By the way, you can still do things like homework checks, taking attendance, and warm-up activities (Early Bird, Daily Oral Language) in the beginning of class, but consider the following approaches instead:

- Make sure warm-up activities ask students to engage with the important concepts of the day's lesson.

- Take attendance while students are engaged with an opening activity. Don't call roll, just note the names of students who are absent.

- Ask students to place the homework on their desks so you can walk around and check it quickly. Make a notation in your grade book to indicate completion not proficiency. You can go over the homework more intensely later in the class period.

If students are struggling to learn, we may not be preparing them properly for learning. A large part of differentiation is dedicated to preparing minds to learn and providing the best environment for that learning to occur. Front-loading and back-loading our lessons with the major concepts we want students to learn is one way to do both of these.

Explore Similarities and Differences, Examples and Nonexamples

Students learn more when they can recognize similarities and differences among terms, objects, and concepts. Teaching them how to identify close and remote connections is one of the most useful differentiation strategies in all disciplines (Marzano, Pickering, and Pollock 2001; Sprenger 2005).

For example, when teaching adverbs, we remind students that not all words that modify other words are adverbs; adjectives modify nouns only, but adverbs modify verbs, adjectives, and other adverbs. We can provide examples and almost-but-not-quite examples (nonexamples) in every subject: What other processes act like phototropism but are actually something else? What makes something an integer versus a noninteger? Are those markings hieroglyphs, petroglyphs, or cuneiform writing, and how did we decide which was which? Frequent and intense experience examining the characteristics of related and unrelated terms makes for powerful long-term memory retention.

Hydration

When students are dehydrated, it's almost as if they are drunk. What they say isn't always clear or relevant to the conversation at hand, they don't make good company, they don't fully engage, they may slump across their desks from fatigue, and they are often cranky. One of the first signs of dehydration while hiking, swimming, or rafting, in fact, is irritability. All of these behaviors make it difficult to learn.

The truth is that students and teachers need to drink water more frequently during the school day than most currently do. After spending an hour in many school buildings with their closed ventilation systems and stale air, students and teachers begin to dehydrate. The myelin sheath that envelops each neuron in the brain must stay hydrated to continue to perform its two tasks: to provide support and protection for the neuron and to conduct the sodium-potassium ion pump that moves the impulse down the length of the axon. Hydrated neurons keep the myelin sheath functioning well, which opens more opportunities for learning. In short, with plentiful water, students' brains work better; if we water them, they will grow.

There are plenty of times when teachers try to entertain or motivate lethargic students, and often resent having to do so. Some teachers bemoan the apathy of today's youth and become irritable themselves. They often get headaches, which they attribute to stress, noise, and lack of sleep. This might be true in some situations, but an overlooked culprit is dehydration.

Provide water breaks every day, whether that means quick trips to the water fountain or letting students bring bottled water or thermoses to class. Because they realize the instructional power and performance impact of hydration, some schools and their business partners provide bottled water for all students on standardized test days.

So give it whirl, what can it hurt? Try drinking water every period you teach. Ask students to do the same. Watch the change in behavior. We may not need to spend as much time scaffolding, tiering, or using other tools of differentiation. In these times, water may be the best way to prime the pump.

Emotional Content

Most new information initially gets processed in the emotional response centers of the adolescent brain. Then the data move to the cognitive centers, and only if a teacher provides developmentally appropriate learning experiences. What this means is that in our classrooms, students typically have an emotional response to our lessons first, and we need to be aware of this tendency and react appropriately. We can't close our minds to this influence and declare, "Just let me teach my curriculum. Don't bother me with the touchy-feely stuff." Attending to the affective connections is crucial to successful differentiation. We can teach something that seems dispassionate, and students will still have an emotional response to it: "This is boring." "This sucks." "This is so unfair." "Just get me through to 2:15." "I wonder if she likes me?" "This is so cool. It fits like a puzzle!" "Oh my gosh, that wasn't on the study guide he gave us yesterday. If he puts that on the test, I'm calling my mom!"

Successful teachers cultivate a classroom environment that is safe and inviting, which reduces students' anxiety and encourages them to learn. Just as teachers purposely plan for homework—"Students will complete problems 2–26 on page 171"—they intentionally create a positive learning environment.

If students feel safe and invited, they feel more comfortable communicating with us about their needs. They are willing to try to new things. They are not threatened by classmates who learn, look, and think differently from them. If the atmosphere is emotionally appropriate, the teacher can be academically appropriate. Try some of the following strategies as you create a safe and inviting classroom that enables effective differentiation:

- Cultivate relationships with students every day. Do not take their attendance or respect for granted. Thank them for participating. (Yes, I know school is compulsory, but students are more motivated when they feel appreciated.) Demonstrate to each of them that they make good company—lean forward and act interested when they talk to you, maintain eye contact (as culturally appropriate), ask about their families and activities, and smile when working with them.

- Talk less and listen more.

- Rather than just praise students, think a little longer about your response, then note what students do and describe the impact it has on the student, you, or the class. For example, instead of, "Great work, Tony!" try, "Tony, you had your materials on the day we needed to use them, and as a result, you and your group finished on time. That really helps!"

- Use students' names in every interaction. It reminds them that they are important to you, and it helps to distinguish them within a large class—an important part of differentiation.

- Find out all you can about your students, then consider that information as you teach them.

- Don't play "gotcha" with students, spending the majority of your time trying to find and correct their mistakes. Seek and affirm their successes.

- Affirm positive risk-taking in the classroom.

- Teach as if you were selling the subject to your students. They need to believe that learning is worth their investment of mind and body.

- Don't punish the whole class because of the actions of a few.

- Ask students to coteach with you.

- Give students leadership responsibilities.

- Be willing to revise your thinking about a student in light of new evidence, such as when a previously uncaring student reaches out to a struggling classmate to get him back on track.

- Make sure students experience real competence in your classroom. This is more than being praised for good work. Students must demonstrate for themselves the skills and knowledge of the day's lessons without wavering too far from the requirements assigned to everyone else. If they don't experience competence regularly, even in small doses, they will find ways to tune you out and, occasionally, get away from the situation (the classroom) using whatever excuse they can find: going to the bathroom, returning a library book, running an errand for you, taking lunch money to the cafeteria, or asking to see a counselor. The brain is a survival organ in terms of energy and dignity (more on this below). If it's threatened, it will often try to find a way to avoid whatever lies ahead.

Novelty

Novelty excites the brain. A break from the routine, a new way to look at an old problem, a different setting or classroom configuration can stimulate learning. Like it or not, teachers today must be aware of how much competition there is for students' attention. We live in an impatient world of sound-bite news, accelerating download speeds, and fast food to go. We have to invest some energy in shaking up the learning environment; we have to keep our lessons fresh.

Instead of always lecturing or writing problems on the overhead projector, you could

- Ask students to teach the lesson with you.

- Incorporate students and their culture in your lesson.

- Ask students to think divergently: "With a partner, work for ten minutes and give me all the arguments against what I just taught you." "Describe the object in five to eight sentences without using a single adjective or adverb." "How are math operation signs like music?"

- Use props in your presentations.

- Make random statements in the middle of your lessons. While teaching fractions, for example, remind students that gravity on the moon is one-sixth that of earth's gravity. "TJ, you could jump over a school bus, and, wow, Marina, you could bat the baseball across town."

- Take unusual field trips in and out of the school building.

- Use simulations, small or large, frequently.

- Incorporate drama. Ask students to interview a historical character; perform a soap-opera love story among electrons as they attach and reattach to one another to create molecules; dress up as the characters in their books and debate the major themes; write and perform fairy tales that incorporate math concepts in the resolutions of their conflicts.

- Add music to the lesson either as background, as an aid to learning, or as the primary focus.

- Teach backwards one day, starting at the end of the lesson and moving to the beginning.

Students' minds get mired in the mundane, and this can dull their thinking. Because young adolescent brains are hard-wired for action, it makes sense to provide unique experiences from time to time to reengage students. Lessons that create curiosity, anticipation, and suspense activate their intellects and direct their physical and emotional energy toward productive goals. When we feed students' natural tendencies for dynamic growth, they not only thrive, they become fully committed to learning.

Meeting Survival Needs

The brain seeks self-preservation. Given a choice, it will always choose to conserve energy and maintain dignity. We are wasting students' time if we try to teach them without trying to meet their needs. This means paying attention to whether they get enough sleep, eat nutritious meals, manage stress, get regular exercise, practice good hygiene, and feel connected to their peers. We can assign daily homework in each of these areas: "Get nine hours of sleep tonight." "Eat five helpings of fruit today." "Break down your homework into ten- to fifteen-minute tasks so it will seem more manageable." "Wash your hands before touching food and after coughing." "Play basketball for forty-five minutes after school." "Join an after-school club or sports program this week." Not every student can or will complete these assignments, but we can make a point of communicating them. We can model many of these good habits for students as well. What's in sight is usually in mind.

We can't always change our students' lives, but we can take reasonable steps to promote healthy habits and keep them safe. If we want students to learn, we must care about their lives in and out of school. What matters to them and what they need to thrive will vary tremendously, and teachers who successfully differentiate pay attention to those distinctions.

One quick point regarding sleep is worth mentioning here. We've all experienced the dreary feeling of working in fluorescent lighting for hours on end, and natural light just seems to be more pleasant and seems to make students more alert. In the classroom, try to keep the window blinds up when showing videos so your students can receive full-spectrum sunlight. If there's a glare on the television or computer screen from the windows, move the students, don't close the blinds. If your classroom is windowless, try to find an incandescent lamp or replace your current fluorescent tubes with full-spectrum fluorescent tubes. They are more expensive and burn warmer than regular ones, but you and your students will not have to fight sleepiness all day long.

Memory Ideas

There are books that offer more wisdom about memory than I can impart here, but successful differentiating teachers try to stay current with new research about how the brain retains information. Check out the Recommended Resources list at the end of the book for some good titles.

Elements of memories are stored in different parts of the brain. If we give students a variety of ways to engage with the topic, we secure a wider network of the memory's storage. It's easier for students to retrieve the memory later.

On a practical level, this can mean encouraging students to draw symbols and connections between ideas while also writing about them. We can create a flow chart of a math algorithm or a scientific process, then ask students to explain the concepts in full sentences and paragraphs. We can ask students to consider a new concept from different points of view, then discuss the varied opinions and later make a craft or product of some sort that represents the perspective closest to their own. As we plan, we seek alternate ways for students to experience new information. If students interact with topics from more than one angle, they will remember it better.

In adolescence, a great deal of mental pruning occurs as neural networks organize themselves. Inactivity can cause the brain to delete and replace old memories. Put another way, every time a neuron fires, it increases the likelihood that it will ignite in the future, and if it doesn't fire for a while, it takes more stimulation and sometimes relearning to restart it. Consequently, teachers must work to spiral the curriculum, visiting and revisiting information all year long. We can't just teach a lesson once and assume students will remember it the rest of the year. Learning requires diligence. One great way to support this premise is through cross-disciplinary applications in which students learn and use skills and concepts in more than one class.

In addition, Sprenger (2005) says reflection and recoding are particularly important to learning. Reflection refers to time, structure, and inclination to pause in one's learning to focus on what is going on. A teacher might respond to a student's contribution to a class discussion with, "Tell me more" and "What else?" We do this each time we ask students to use learning logs, summarizations, journal prompts, and interactive notebooks.

Recoding refers to the way students put knowledge into their own constructs. These can be symbolic, abstract, or physical. Students recode when they categorize and structure information; associate visual images with knowledge; make inferences, comparisons, and contrasts; and explain ideas to others (Sprenger 2005, 61–66).

Pat Wolfe (2001) tells us that the human brain has a limited number of unrelated items that it can recall simultaneously, depending on the person's age. For example, five-year-olds can best remember two unrelated items or facts at a time. Middle school students are usually comfortable with five or fewer facts, and high school students can juggle about seven simultaneously. So, as we present material, we can use these guidelines to maximize what students learn: "What are two things we learned about clouds today?" "Let's list five differences between these two periods of history." "What are the seven steps in this molecular evolution?"

One final thought on memory: We file by similarity, but we retrieve by difference (Sousa 2005). If two factors are closely associated in our minds, we try to store them together—the brain loves connections. But when we try to pull the information from our minds, we search for it according to unique identifiers—the differences.

Filing by similarity can cause problems with commonly confused concepts such as rotation/revolution, simile/metaphor, area/perimeter, osmosis/diffusion, renaissance/medieval, and I/me. These concepts tend to blur together in our minds if they are not distinct enough from each other. Students may think they have distinguished between two similar ideas or objects, but in reality, they have troubled remembering which one is which. When asked to circle similes in text, for example, they circle anything that falls under the figurative language umbrella: similes, metaphors, personification, allegory, and vivid descriptions.

If students are going to be easily confused by two or more similar concepts, we should separate the lessons by a few days. If time doesn't allow us to do that, we emphasize the differences and not the similarities and give students plenty of opportunity to practice discriminating between the two.

Social Interaction

The brain is innately social (Sousa 2005). It requires interaction to remember things well. One of the best ways we can help students retain information is to engage them in substantive conversations about their learning.

Consider how you might increase the ways students make oral connections with content and skills. Although this is crucial for students with strong interpersonal intelligence, it's also vital to every student's learning. Instead of another session listening to a lecture, answering questions after a reading, or filling out a graphic organizer, how about asking students to talk about their learning in a structured manner?

Two more ideas are pertinent here. First, whoever is responding to students in the classroom is doing the majority of learning. Think about that for a moment. Who responds to students' contributions in a typical classroom? The teacher does. The teacher asks a question, the student responds, and it is the teacher who declares whether or not the student is correct or asks follow-up or clarifying questions. The teacher does a lot of learning.

Wait a minute! The teacher supposedly knows the material already; it's the students who are supposed to be learning. We need to reverse the ratio.

As often as possible, arrange for classmates to respond to classmates. Rather than declaring something a student says right or wrong, ask another student to give evidence to support or refute the opinion, then ask a third student to critique the second student's evidence. Call on the original student to offer a rebuttal. Step in only to prevent misconceptions from taking root and to call on different students.

Will this approach have much of an impact the first time we use it? Probably not. We may need to do it several times before students fully grasp the pattern. The benefit is that students will continue accessing those neural pathways after a question is posed instead of shutting down; they will expect a follow-up inquiry.

Second, differentiation expert Betty Hollas (2006) reports that in a typical classroom, teachers ask eighty questions for every two questions posed by students. More disturbing, 80 percent of those questions are at the lowest levels of Bloom's Taxonomy—recall and comprehension. Once again, we have to reverse these ratios. We must encourage and enable students to ask more questions of us and each other—certainly more than we ask of them. And we must improve the quality of the questions. This means making classroom conversational inquiry habitual and compelling. Every day, we should provide time for practice question-asking.

"Working with a partner, brainstorm as many questions as you can to which the answer is homeostasis."

"Identify four equations using exponents and square roots to which the solution is 15."

"If artist Henri Matisse is the answer, what's the question?"

To make our subjects compelling enough to generate questions, create curiosity every day. Here are a few ideas:

- Ask students to conduct intelligent conversations without using verbs.

- Place a closed box with objects inside that are to be used later in the lesson in the center of the room and place warning and danger stickers all over it. What might be inside and why is it here?

- As you close your lesson, foreshadow the next day's lesson: "Tomorrow we'll see how scientists in ancient Egypt actually helped our modern astronauts do their jobs."

- Using VELCRO, attach props to your clothing that you will work into the lesson.

- Facilitate more constructivist approaches in which students identify a question they want to ask and develop the methodology to answer it. Inquiry labs and research reports fit well here.

- Before reading expository text, play with the ideas via manipulatives or verbal sparring with students. For example, before talking about bioluminescence in phytoplankton, videotape or describe what it's like to walk along the sand at night in places such as northern California where the pressure of our feet can leave green-glowing footprints on the beach, compliments of the plankton in the sand. Before reading about immigration issues and NAFTA in relation to individuals coming from Mexico, engage students in a conversation about the history of relations between the two nations, particularly about the portion of our history when the United States took large portions of territory away from Mexico by force to create what is now much of the southwest region of the United States.

  Reveal portions of a new concept a little at a time, reminding students that more is to come. This heightens their sense of anticipation and primes their brains for questions. Metaphorically, this is like lifting the corner of a tarpaulin that covers a painting or solving a section of a jigsaw puzzle without knowing what the full picture will be. As part of a lesson, you might provide a sample of a dramatic scene from the Canterbury Tales, then later share a romantic scene and ask students to wonder about the connections. You could "lift the tarpaulin" a bit by showing them translations from ancient Egyptian text that indicate sophisticated understanding of astronomy and suggest that this is just the beginning of the surprises about Egypt to be discovered in the unit ahead.

- Get started asking questions, then let the students run with them. For example, at the beginning of a unit about grammar rules, you might ask students to create their own language. Typically they will spend their time building an alphabet code with new symbols that correlate to each letter. They might provide a few translated sentences and claim they are done. Don't let them stop there! After they've shared their code, start asking questions. "How do you create plural endings in your language?" "How about past, present, and future tenses?" "What about numbers?" "How about the end of one thought and the beginning of another?" Then ask them to generate other questions that someone learning their new language would want to know.

Chapter 5

Twelve Samples of Differentiated Learning Experiences from Multiple Subjects

The lesson and sequence described in Chapter 2 was fairly intense. Successful differentiated lessons can require a lot of planning. Being proactive is very helpful, but there will be occasions when even our best planning fails to account for all that happens in the classroom. As differentiating teachers we are responsive teachers who remain flexible so we can adapt to the changing needs and circumstances of our students. In sum, we still have to differentiate as warranted if lessons don't go according to plan.

Let's examine a dozen scenarios from a variety of grade levels and curriculum areas to see how we might augment or revise them when the original lesson proves insufficient.

Keep in mind that the suggested strategies are just starting points. These ideas will spark your own ideas. In addition, some of the ideas may work well in more than one scenario and in multiple subjects, so I've listed them more than once. We wouldn't want to limit the use of a good idea in a new situation just because we used it once with a small group in a previous situation.

SCENARIO 1 NEWTON'S FIRST LAW

Some science students can recite Newton's First Law (an object at rest or in motion stays at rest or in motion unless acted upon by an external force) from memory, but they are not able to describe it or apply it well.

Differentiation Strategies

We can create an anchor activity for the rest of the class, then move these struggling students to one side and provide several ten-to-fifteen-minute experiences designed to deepen their understanding of Newton's First Law over several days. For one experience, we could place a playground ball on a large board or tray. Make sure the surface isn't slanted. When the ball is stable (at rest), ask students to watch the ball for two minutes or more to see if it moves. When it doesn't move after the allotted time period, ask students to draw a conclusion about whether the ball would move if all the conditions stayed the same day after day, week after week, and year after year. They should conclude that the ball would not move.

Next, ask students what it would take for the ball to move. Responses will likely include someone hitting it, another object hitting it, an explosion underneath the ball, and tilting the board on which it rests. Point out to students that these are all actions. What can they now conclude about an object at rest and what it takes to move it? Our hope is that they will conclude that "an object at rest will stay at rest unless something acts upon it" or something similar.

Now tilt the board to one side and watch the ball roll off the surface. Ask students what force (action) caused the ball to move? "Gravity," would be the best response here, of course. When the ball hits the floor, ask students what stopped the ball from continuing its path or trajectory (the floor and perhaps, later, the wall against which it stopped). As it rolls to one side and eventually stops, ask students to identify what other forces are acting upon it now to stop its motion (gravity, an object in its path, or friction with the floor). Finally ask them to restate Newton's First Law.

On subsequent days, provide more demonstrations or experiences with Newton's First Law, each time asking students to explain the law. For some students, you might show NASA footage from inside the space shuttle of astronauts playing with objects in zero gravity. When they push on an object, for example, there is no force acting upon it except for the gentle friction with air molecules. Objects go spinning along their trajectory until they hit the bulkhead or another object. The astronauts' body movements demonstrate the principles of Newton's First Law.

Dr. William C. Robertson has a great demonstration involving a marble and an old Hot Wheels plastic track piece in his wonderful book *Stop Faking It! Force and Motion*. Just imagine creating a vertical **J** shape with the bendable Hot Wheels track, rolling the marble from the short side of the **J**-curve and measuring how high up the other side the marble rolls. Then imagine how it may or may not change the distance rolled as you lowered the longer, vertical side of the **J** halfway down, then all the way down into a slightly curved **L** shape. What would stop the marble from rolling forever once it hits the horizontal, flat part of the **L**?

In each demonstration or example, ask students to explain what's going on and to restate Newton's Law orally and in writing. Finally, ask them to find at least two examples from their daily lives that demonstrate this law. Brainstorm a list of possibilities if they need some direction.

General Differentiation Strategies Employed

- Make abstract concepts vivid, concrete experiences.

- Use repetition.

- Increase the number of processing techniques—visual, auditory, and written.

- Use anchor activity mini-lessons.

- Use temporary, homogeneous grouping.

SCENARIO 2 SUMS OF INTERIOR ANGLES

Math students are learning that the sum of the interior angles of a quadrilateral (such as a square, rectangle, trapezoid, parallelogram, and rhombus) equals 360 degrees, and the sum of the interior angles of a triangle equals 180 degrees. Some students have just memorized the formula quickly without really understanding how it works, some understand it well, some are still struggling with language issues, and some are ready to move on to the next level of understanding.

Differentiation Strategies

Using the football metaphor to structure the lesson, first lead the whole class through a review of these concepts with whatever approach seems most appropriate. But when processing information in the more expanded portion of the lesson, provide experiences for the four different groups: students on grade level, students whose primary language is not English, students who are struggling with the concepts, and advanced students.

Processing task(s) for students on grade level

Provide multiple practice problems in which students take three-sided and four-sided shapes with some of the interior angle measurements identified and use those measurements to determine the measurements of the remaining angles.

Provide multiple practice problems in which students use the write-ups of how some students solved problems similar to the ones above and determine whether or not they were successful. If errors were made, students can identify them and describe how to correct them.

Processing task(s) for struggling students

Give students multiple practice experiences in which they use a protractor to measure the interior angles of differently sized quadrilaterals and triangles. They record the data in a chart, such as the following:

Shape (T = Triangle) (Q = Quadrilateral)	Angle 1	Angle 2	Angle 3	Angle 4 (if applicable)	Total of All Angle Measurements
1 (T)					
2 (T)					
3 (T)					
4 (Q)					
5 (Q)					
6 (Q)					

After the students have completed the chart, ask them to search for patterns in the totals according to shape. Then ask students to find the measurements of the interior angles of several triangles and record the sum of the angles. After they have recorded these totals, ask students to remove any one side of their triangles, then add two lines to create a quadrilateral. Ask them to measure and record the sum of the interior angles of these new quadrilaterals.

Processing task(s) for advanced students

Ask students to find the totals of the interior angles of pentagons and hexagons, then to determine if there is a standard total for the sum of these angles as with quadrilaterals and triangles.

After they have completed this sequence, ask students to write down the steps they took to figure it out.

Processing task(s) for students struggling with language only

Ask students to write two different fictitious pages from a textbook that explain how to determine the sum of the interior angles of triangles and quadrilaterals—one in their native language and one a translation of that page.

Ask students to solve two math problems in which they are given a shape and the measurements of only some of the interior angles. Students must determine the measure of the remaining angles. After they have completed this step, ask them to explain their solutions, step by step, to a student who is fluent in English.

Ask students to write the following words and numbers in the shape of their meaning: *angle, interior, triangle, quadrilateral, right* (as in right angle), *perpendicular, 180 degrees, 360 degrees, sum, square, rectangle, trapezoid, parallelogram, rhombus.* For example, *perpendicular* and *180 degrees* could be written as

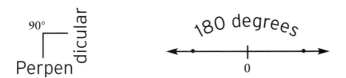

When groups have finished these tasks, bring everyone back together to review the major concepts in whatever manner seems most appropriate for the group.

General Differentiation Strategies Employed

- Provide tiered lessons, according to readiness levels.

- Conduct error analysis.

- Adjust practice experiences.

- Guide practice.

- Use manipulatives.

- Use graphic organizers to clarify and to provide a structured approach.

- Move from known to unknown.

- Use constructivism.

SCENARIO 3 LEARNING FROM LECTURES

Students are not able to retain much from your lectures.

Differentiation Strategies

Lectures can be wonderful teaching tools if done well. Lectures in which the speaker unfolds a narrative in a compelling way are among the most remembered. Not all of us can do this consistently, of course, so it's not wise to rely on lecturing as our prime, instructional method. We should vary our approaches.

Consider using more think-pair-share activities, reflective questioning, demonstrations, debates, manipulatives, compare-and-contrast experiences, and constructivism in which students are guided to make their own discoveries.

When students have to cull what's important from what's trivial on their own without any immediate feedback, they often give up because the task seems so daunting. This happens a lot during lectures. To keep students from disengaging, provide a T-chart or graphic organizer so they can fill in the missing information during breaks in the lecture. We can also give them a printout of the notes with a few missing pieces here and there. During the breaks, students fill in key headings, vocabulary terms, and other pieces. Give these structures to students ahead of time and ask them to specifically listen for mention of these items. Instead of having to determine what's important on their own, students respond to a prompt in the form of the visual metaphor, the organizer.

Check to see if you are asking students to do anything, such as taking notes, during the lecture. If so, stop. We diminish the impact of both the lecture and the note-taking experience when we ask students to do both simultaneously. Ask students to pay careful attention to the lecture—pens and pencils down—then provide short breaks every ten to fifteen minutes to allow them to process what they've heard and considered in their notes before resuming the lecture.

Prime students' minds for learning. At the beginning of lectures, identify what students should learn through listening.

Some students will need additional lessons about how to take accurate notes. Make sure to show students examples of strong as well as flawed note-taking strategies. Show students samples of outstanding results on assessments taken with the use of notes as well as mediocre results obtained when students did not take and use notes from a lecture.

General Differentiation Strategies Employed

- Use alternative instructional methods.

- Vary the structures for diverse readiness levels.

- Prime the brain for learning.

- Provide examples.

- Conduct mini-lessons for specific skills.

SCENARIO 4 PHYSICAL EDUCATION SKILLS

Some students in a physical education class cannot participate fully due to their limited development or poor health.

Differentiation Strategies

Start small. Identify the individual movements or steps to whatever you're teaching, and ask students to practice these. For example, before asking students to run a mile or other lengthy distance, show them how to warm up for intensive exercise. Let them practice this several times. We also need to teach students how to begin an endurance task, as well as how to pace themselves. Some students may combine running and walking initially, but later in the year they may change the ratio to include more running than walking. Some students may need help with their mental state as they begin and maintain such a rigorous program of exercise.

Assess students against their own personal improvement goals, not against goals set for all students at this age level. Help students create a baseline of performance data, then grade them based on the progress they make toward their goals.

Let struggling students use tools early in the learning, then slowly remove the props. For example, when learning how to swim, students initially might use hand paddles or some kind of floating device to keep their legs near the surface of the water. Over time, they can practice swimming greater distances without these props.

Increase the amount and type of feedback for struggling students and make sure to offer suggestions in a timely manner that enables them to use the information to improve. Weekly, if not daily, formative assessment and feedback have dramatic impact on students' achievement.

Give students more time to develop physically before holding them accountable for the same level of performance. Personal story: I was big-boned and tall in middle school, but I wasn't strong. My friends could all do more than eight pull-ups, but I couldn't do one. By the tenth grade, however, my muscles caught up with my height, and I could do eight or more pull-ups just like everyone else. A teacher back in my middle school years who differentiated instruction might have recognized that I wasn't developmentally ready for this form of exercise and set up a program to help me progress. That didn't happen, however, and I felt like a castaway, often using humor to hide the fact that I couldn't do what my classmates could. Although I excelled academically in middle school, in my head I was a loser.

Did it really matter in the big scheme of things that I could not do eight pull-ups until the tenth grade? No. I don't want any of my students to feel the same way I did, especially when achievement is so attainable in just a few months or years under a thoughtful teacher's guidance, and when self-worth can and should come from more than just the number of pull-ups one can do.

General Differentiation Strategies Employed

- Adjust the pacing of instruction; make it developmentally appropriate.
- Use feedback.
- Adjust student's goals.
- Work in small increments.
- Allow the use of developmental tools.

SCENARIO 5 ART SKILLS

Students in your art class have minimal skills, and you're concerned they won't be able to meet the course requirements.

Differentiation Strategies

We can break down more complex skills into smaller steps and give students extended practice with each skill. For example, if an assignment asks students to create a clay sculpture by attaching multiple pieces of clay, show them how to score the surface of small pieces of clay (roughing up the surfaces of the two clay pieces, applying water to each surface, and attaching the pieces along these surfaces), then ask them to score and attach progressively larger pieces of clay.

Consider possible misconceptions and identify at least two steps you can take to prevent them. For example, if you're teaching about contour lines, some students may not be able to identify them by just looking at an object on display. To meet these students' needs, consider projecting the image of an object on a screen, tracing the contour outline on the newsprint behind the projected image, then remove the projection, leaving only the contour behind. Students can practice this on their own with several objects before being asked to focus on contours in the context of the lesson.

Give students a chance to do every project two times or more. Some students may need several weeks to shape and revise an art project until they have achieved the standards and can submit their work for a grade.

There are other things we can do, such as setting more developmentally appropriate goals for these students and assessing them against their progression toward these goals. We can ask an adult volunteer to work individually with struggling students. We can extend the deadline for these students to submit their work or ask them to come after school for some additional practice and instruction. And we can provide practice materials that they can take home and use.

General Differentiation Strategies Employed

- Adjust learning goals.

- Allow repetition.

- Provide alternative routes to the same level of mastery.

- Break larger tasks into smaller ones.

- Extend deadlines.

- Provide additional practice.

- Involve a mentor.

- Provide necessary tools for learning.

- Address misconceptions.

SCENARIO 6 SIMPLIFYING SQUARE ROOTS

Some students are struggling with how to simplify square roots. For example, $\sqrt{80}$ is the square root of 80 factored into perfect squares and remaining factors: 16×5, or $4 \times 4 \times 5$. Note that each 4 is a perfect square of 2, and there are two of these perfect squares. When we simplify it, we see that we have the square roots of 4, 4, and 5 to consider, and all but the 5 are perfect squares. The 5, then, stays under the radical sign while the perfect squares (the 4s) come out. Simplified, the answer is $2 \times 2 \times \sqrt{5}$, or $4\sqrt{5}$. In another example, $\sqrt{32y^7}$ can be simplified to $4y^3\sqrt{2y}$. See the box for the steps of this process.

$$\sqrt{32y^7} = \sqrt{4 \times 4 \times 2 \times y \times y \times y \times y \times y \times y \times y}$$
$$= 2 \times 2\sqrt{2 \times y^2 \times y^2 \times y^2 \times y}$$
$$= 4y^3\sqrt{2y}$$

Differentiation Strategies

Remind struggling students that the square root of any number squared is that number. For example, the square root of 3 squared is 3 (or, $\sqrt{3^2} = 3$). When we simplify square roots, we're taking them down to their basic levels in which everything under the radical sign that's a perfect square is moved to the outside of the radical sign, leaving only nonperfect squares under the radical sign. Understanding that the square root of any number squared is that number ($\sqrt{n^2} = n$) will help students identify and remove perfect squares from under the radical sign.

Give struggling students extra practice simplifying square roots with perfect squares such as 4, 9, 16, and 25; with nonperfect squares (squares that don't come out so evenly, such as 32, 48, and 60—there's always a remainder after the perfect squares are removed); and square roots with variables (such as y squared or cubed). Make sure each one requires students to factor out any perfect squares under the radical sign.

Ask students to share strategies and discuss possible differences in their responses.

Ask students to create a flow chart or sequence map of the steps one takes to simplify square roots. For some students, you'll have to demonstrate how to create a flow chart with several examples.

Show students a visual portrayal of squares by using graph paper. For example, students can count the boxes in the area below and see that the three-by-three grid creates an area of nine squares:

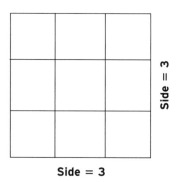

Side = 3

To get the area of a square, we multiply side by side: In this case, $3 \times 3 =$ 9. To find the root of the square (square root), then, we look at the length of one side of the square.

For the tilted square below, students are given each side of the square as $\sqrt{2}$, then asked to determine the total area of the square. Side times side, or $\sqrt{2} \times \sqrt{2}$, equals $\sqrt{4}$, and since this is a perfect square, we can remove the 4 from under the radical and simplify the expression as just 2.

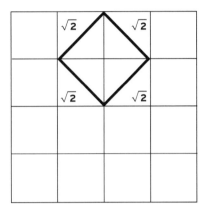

Give students plenty of practice finding the square roots and the squares using visual cues such as these.

Allow some students to retake the quiz on this material for full credit if they fail the first quiz. It may take them longer to master it.

Special thanks to Lorie Banks in Holyoke, Massachusetts, for assistance with these ideas.

General Differentiation Strategies Employed

- Connect new concepts with familiar ones.

- Break concepts down to smaller steps.

- Provide additional practice.

- Provide visual cues.

- Conduct error analysis.

- Anticipate misconceptions and take steps to prevent them.

- Create a road map or flow chart of the steps involved.

- Allow for the fact that not all students will learn at the same pace as their classmates, and give students every chance to demonstrate mastery, not just one chance. Allow retakes for full credit.

SCENARIO 7 EDITING TEXT

Some students are not catching all the mistakes in grammar and punctuation when they edit.

Differentiation Strategies

Ask students to edit very short sentences at first, progressing to longer ones.

Ask students to find only major errors such as forgetting to capitalize proper names or the first word of a sentence. Then ask them to edit more subtle mistakes such as when to use a semicolon or proper spacing after a period when typing.

Do not edit these students' papers. Instead, place a dot at the end of any line that contains an editing error, and ask them to find and correct the error.

Ask students to edit in waves. The first time they will read through the text for spelling issues. The second time they will look for capitalization problems. The third time they will look for comma usage. The fourth time, noun-verb agreements. Each "wave" of reading through the text adds a different skill.

Ask struggling students to analyze the editing work of their peers.

Provide some of these students with additional editing practice.

Play a few editing games in which students win points by catching the editing mistakes of others. Award prizes such as a copy of Strunk and White's *Elements of Style*, Great Source's *Writer's, Inc.*, a dictionary, a thesaurus, a crazy pen, or a book on how to publish one's writing.

Encourage students to find mistakes in your writing, whether on a handout or on the chalkboard, and if they find any errors, reward them and publicly affirm their skills.

Provide a series of simple and compound sentences, and ask students to incorporate different punctuation marks that change the meaning in at least three different ways. Then ask them to identify which punctuation approach is most appropriate, given the paragraphs in which they are found.

Ask students to compare the rules of proper written communication such as punctuation, capitalization, usage, spelling, and agreement, with the rules they find when writing text messages on their cell phones, PDAs, or computers. FWIW WE NEED 2 LRN THEIR SOP ASAP OR WE'LL BE F2F W/PPL WE DON'T NO. CRAZY, THAT. F/HW TRW APPS, IT'S CHANGING. BYKT. RU READY FOR NEW POV? YBB. EOL/L8R. *Translation:* For what it's worth, we need to learn their way of doing things (standard operating procedure) as soon as possible, or we will be facing (face to face with) students (people) we don't know. It's crazy to think about learning all this, I know. From homework to real-world applications, things are changing. But you knew that. Are you ready for these new points of view? You better be. End of lecture. Later.

General Differentiation Strategies Employed

- Relate new knowledge to students' world view—relevancy.

- Work in gradations, moving from introductory-level understanding to more sophisticated levels.

- Apply the knowledge in new ways.

- Guide students' own discoveries rather than telling them what to do directly.

- Conduct error analysis.

- Provide additional practice.

- Increase friendly competition.

SCENARIO 8 SHOW, DON'T TELL

Students are at different levels of readiness when it comes to showing, not just telling, in their writing.

Differentiation Strategies

For students who are on grade level, provide multiple opportunities to practice. For example, show students simple sentences such as those below, and ask them to describe the intended object without using the modifier.

It was raining hard.	It was a difficult decision.
I was afraid.	She was excited.
The river was full.	It was a boring afternoon.
The classroom was busy.	The dog looked dangerous.
The map was ancient.	

Students should use whatever strategies you taught them in the introductory lesson to do this. Here's an example of what they might write, based on the original sentence "The rainforest was humid."

Moisture dripped from the large, bowed banana leaves, then fell the short distance to the thick soil of the forest floor. Every few minutes Gabriel peeled his shirt away from his torso. The sweat on his face gathered in small rivers and flowed downward, following the curve of his eyebrows and cheekbones. Breathing was like sucking mud through a straw; he hoped at least once he'd get a pocket of cold, fresh air, but each inhale was the same—wet and full of mildew. Hiking up the steep incline toward the Mayan ruins turned his leg muscles to overcooked noodles. He stopped and unfolded the map for the third time and noted his fingers were wrinkled, like they are after a long shower or swim.

Never once in the description do we describe the rainforest as humid. We show the reader, not tell the reader.

For advanced students, ask them to engage in similar activities using descriptions that are more complex and less vivid.

The software was intricate.
Her argument was nuanced.
There wasn't another law like it.
He was more reserved in his appraisal.
It was a snow job from the start.
Kirby reveled in Jen's existential fortitude.

These students can also help design the evaluative criteria to be used when critiquing the success of a student's attempts to show, not tell, in writing.

For struggling students, we can provide descriptions from the novels they are currently reading and ask them to identify what makes a particular passage successful or mediocre. We can provide several think-aloud activities, with both teacher and students reflecting in front of the class. We can provide additional feedback after each attempt is made. As a subskill focus, we can also ask students to practice rewriting sentences in different ways while preserving the meaning.

- Lakeisha ate a slice of pizza.

- Lakeisha sank her teeth deep into the pizza's cheese.

- Realizing how long she had been without food, Lakeisha inhaled the slice.

- A small rivulet of grease rolled lazily down the contours of Lakeisha's chin as she took bite after bite of the Chicago pie.

General Differentiation Strategies Employed

- Focus on specific skills.

- Provide examples and nonexamples of the goal.

- Adjust the level of complexity.

- Provide extended practice.

- Provide additional feedback to those first learning the topic.

- Provide ample think-alouds to model successful thinking.

SCENARIO 9 CALCULATING SIMPLE INTEREST

Some students do not understand how to calculate simple interest on an investment, such as in the following example:

Simple interest = Principal × Rate × Number of years

Invest $5,000 at 10% for 4 years: $5,000 × .10 × 4 = $2,000

Add this to the original investment, $5,000, to obtain the total in the account of $7,000.

Differentiation Strategies

Provide several think-aloud experiences by both teachers and classmates so students can see and hear clear modeling of what to do.

Provide answers to problems, and ask students how they would find the solutions.

Ask students to orally walk a classmate through the problem, explaining what they did to solve it.

Provide incorrect solutions, and ask students to identify the errors and correct them.

Provide a flow chart that tracks the sequence students would go through to determine simple interest on a loan.

Connect the correct calculation to real-life—why would someone want to be able to do this?

Ask students to compare different amounts of money invested at different rates and for varying amounts of time to determine the best investment among the group.

Do a mini-simulation. Provide fake dollars, and ask students to "invest" them in your fake bank for a few days. Allow them to choose from several different investment options, such as 5 percent for three days, 8 percent for two days, and 10 percent for one day. Using each day as a fictitious year, return their fake money with the interest earned. Ask students to compare their results.

As students progress, ask them to find other elements of the formula. For example, we may not have all the information in the way we want it or we may be looking for different things. Life is messy, and sometimes we have to think flexibly. If we want to know how much money we need to invest in order to achieve a particular financial goal, we'll have to tackle simple interest differently.

How much principal needs to be invested at 6% interest that will yield $3,000 in four years?

Principal (P) $\times$ .06 $\times$ 4 = $3,000

P $\times$ 0.24 = $3,000

P = $3,000 / .24

P = $12,500

$12,500 needs to be invested

After they have completed a few of these examples, they can figure out the rate and the number of years in varying situations as well. Periodically ask these students to explain to you or a classmate their thinking as they work out the problems.

General Differentiation Strategies Employed

- Increase the task complexity.

- Provide opportunities for students to think flexibly.

- Connect the academic task to real-world applications.

- Use think-alouds.

- Ask students to work backwards from the final solution to the original problem.

- Model the process.

- Provide visual prompts (flow charts) to aid their understanding.

- Use simulations.

SCENARIO 10 ATOMIC STRUCTURE

Some students understand atomic structure quickly (each atom has a nucleus with protons and neutrons, and electrons orbit in shells outside the nucleus) after the first day of instruction, but most of the class is still learning the terms and the general model.

Protons: *positively charged particles in the nucleus*

Neutrons: *chargeless (neither positive nor negative) particles in the nucleus*

Electrons: *negatively charged particles in clouds around the nucleus*

Atomic number: *number of protons in one atom*

Mass number: *the amount of matter in an object (the sum of the number of protons and neutrons in a nucleus of one isotope of an element)*

Isotopes: *atoms with the same atomic number but different mass numbers (atoms with different numbers of neutrons)*

Differentiation Strategies

For struggling students, explain that the atomic structure you're teaching is a metaphor for something we cannot see. In fact, we have never actually seen this structure with the aided or unaided eye, but we know it exists because everything else makes sense when using this foundational understanding; we can see the clear effects of this structure, not the structure itself. If time allows, pose questions about what happens at the subatomic level (moving our focus to the behaviors of the tiniest components of the nucleus), such as we find in the field of quantum mechanics. Even struggling students can grasp the idea that we cannot know an electron's precise location and its momentum at the same moment (Heisenberg's Uncertainty Principle). We can even help students use the "cloud" of probability as a good metaphor for where those electrons are.

Ask these students to build models of specific atoms, labeling the protons, electrons, and neutrons. In addition, they can look at diagrams that reveal the structures of different atoms and identify any errors. Ask students to explore the impact of the positive and negative charges—attracting and repelling each other—and consider what would happen if one charge exceeded another or if both charges were equal.

You can also ask these students to work in small groups and create a pantomime of an atom's general structure. After each group presents, ask the rest of the class to critique the presenting group in terms of accuracy and completeness. Finally, ask students to categorize atoms of different elements according to their structures (diagrams provided by you).

For students who already understand the basic atomic structure, provide them with text, diagrams, and computer animation indicating how atomic structure changes when atoms are combined into molecules. Start with recognizable connections such as hydrogen and oxygen combining to create H_2O, water. Ask these students to create models of the molecules and explain them orally to classmates.

Advanced students can also research specific questions they have about atomic structure in general or about subatomic levels. Of particular interest to many students is the theory of relativity. Some students will find value in connecting the theory to what they know of atomic structure. Let them pursue deeper interest in the topic.

General Differentiation Strategies Employed

- Explain the metaphor we use to teach concepts.

- Provide physical models and experiences of abstract concepts.

- Stimulate and build upon students' curiosity.

- Start with what students know and move to what they don't yet know.

- Allow students to move ahead in the curriculum if they have already mastered the current portion.

SCENARIO 11 TAXONOMIC REFERENCES WITH ENGLISH LANGUAGE LEARNERS

Some English language learners are having trouble memorizing the proper sequence of taxonomic references, such as:

Kingdom

Phylum

Class

Order

Family

Genus

Species

and within kingdoms, the five major kingdoms: Monera (blue-green algae, bacteria), Protista (unicellular, like protozoa, some algae and slime molds), Fungi (molds, mushrooms, yeasts), Plantae, Animalia.

An investigation into whether I should list five or six kingdoms of life in this scenario resulted in a complex chase for a clear answer. A similar investigation by more advanced students in your class would help them see that sometimes the "facts" laid out in textbooks are not always so hard and fast. Try starting an investigation at the website of the Tree of Life Project: http://tolweb.org/Life_on_Earth/1.

Differentiation Strategies

Incorporate Gardner's multiple intelligences theory. For example, students who have strong interpersonal skills might conduct a conversation with a classmate using the scientific terms. Let them use their notes.

Student 1: Phylum groupings fit within the larger Kingdom category.
Student 2: Yes, I know that, and there are five major kingdoms.
Student 1: The first three are: Monera, Protista, and Fungi. Can you name the other two?
Student 2: Yes, they are the easiest to remember—plants and animals, Plantae and Animalia.
Student 1: Can you name the Kingdom, Phylum, Class, Order, Family, Genus, and Species for any one animal?
Student 2: Yes, I can, but I'm going to make a mistake on purpose. You tell me the mistake.

Kingdom: Animalia
Phylum: Arthropoda
Class: Mammalia
Order: Carnivora
Family: Felidae
Genus: *Felis*
Species: *domesticus*

Student 1: That's easy. Felidae? Felis? Feline? It's a cat. It's not an arthropod with segmented bodies and appendages attached to each section, like a tarantula. The phylum was the one that was wrong.

Teach students to invent an appropriate and easily memorable mnemonic to recall the sequence of the taxonomy. For taxonomy: "<u>K</u>ing <u>P</u>eter <u>C</u>ooks <u>O</u>reos <u>F</u>or <u>G</u>oofy <u>S</u>pies." For kingdoms: "<u>M</u>any <u>P</u>eople <u>F</u>ind <u>P</u>lants <u>A</u>mazing."

Write the level of the taxonomies on index cards and ask students to sort them quickly. Turn this into a game for two or more teams.

Write each taxonomy category on an index card folded in half and hang the cards over a string suspended across the classroom. Mix up the order and ask individual students to move the cards to correct the sequence.

Ask students to write each word in the shape of its meaning. You can also ask students to write each word as an umbrella over the one below it, so they can see one is within the other.

Give students the names of animals and ask them to research and plot the proper names for each level for specific animals on a taxonomic chart or dichotomous key. Give them at least five different life forms so they get plenty of practice.

General Differentiation Strategies Employed

- Incorporate Gardner's multiple intelligences theory.

- Use mnemonics.

- Teach students to categorize information.

- Turn abstract ideas into physical manifestations.

- Provide extended practice.

SCENARIO 12 STUDENTS CAN'T SIT STILL

Certain students aren't able to sit still during extended learning experiences such as listening to a lecture or presentation, watching an information video, waiting their turn during classroom discussion and games, graphing a lot of data, or conducting quiet, individual research in the library. During these times they're either talking to classmates, calling out of turn, passing notes, laughing, getting out of their seats to run unnecessary errands, or digging into the edge of their desks with a paperclip or pen.

Differentiation Strategies

These students may not be aware of how distracting they are to others and their own learning. Of course, they may be aware of how distracting they are but may not have the tools needed to change their behavior. There are many steps we can take to help them find ways to curb their impulsive conduct, which will help the rest of the class as well.

We need to find out why these students are acting on impulse so often. How do they behave in other classes and situations? Do they require more than the average amount of attention? Are they hyperactive because of diet or medicine? Can they not respond to social cues appropriately? Can they not read well, and their behavior is an effort to cover this deficiency? Are they getting enough exercise each day and sleeping well at night? Are their families going through a rough time at home? Is the material too easy, making them bored?

If students are not aware of how they distract themselves and others from learning, we need to help them understand the impact of their actions. This should be done discreetly, not publicly or in an admonishing tone. We can talk to them about it, and if that doesn't work, we can also videotape a short segment of the class period and play it back for them privately during a break later in the day, asking them to describe the behavior and how it affected them and their classmates. It can be really hard for adolescents to accept the impact of their actions, particularly at the stage of life when the ego looms large. But videotapes don't lie.

If students consistently speak out of turn, we can give them speaking allotments. For example, we can affirm their excellent contributions but explain that others need a chance to speak as well. In the current discussion, we might limit their speech to four times. After that, they must keep quiet, so they will want to choose their moments wisely. Or, using another structure, students may speak as many times as they want, but only after three students have spoken in turn. We can work out a private signal with them that indicates they're pushing the limits of proper behavior and need to settle down.

We can provide preferential seating for students so they will be seated near the teacher and/or surrounded by "buffer" students who are not easily distracted.

Nothing motivates like success, and we can make sure that all students experience success, no matter how small. If students are motivated, they won't act inappropriately unless there is a severe physiological condition beyond the normal adolescent tendency toward impulsivity.

We can provide a small basket of items with which students can "fiddle" as they listen. These items might include small plastic Slinkies (the metal ones make too much noise), Koosh balls, and stress balls as well as tessellations and others patterns that can be traced with colored pencils or markers. These items create an effect similar to background white noise that diffuses students' excess energy in a way that keeps them focused on the lecture, demonstration, or other learning experience without needing to talk out of turn or act impulsively.

Distracting students can also be woven into the lesson's delivery. They can coteach with us, assist in a demonstration, lead small groups, and help prepare the lesson, all of which keeps them invested in the lesson's success.

We'll need to be mindful to let the distracting students practice new behaviors in short chunks, too. This means that we'll need to establish behavior parameters for these students and have them practice in short time periods. For example, if we want to minimize students' impulsivity, we could start by asking them to remain silent for two minutes, then let them talk. Two minutes might not sound like a long time to an adult, but to adolescents practicing a new behavior, it can be a very long stretch. Later, we might ask them to keep quiet for four minutes and keep building. Eventually we'll figure out suitable parameters. During this progression, such students might take three steps forward for every two steps backward, but that's expected.

We can also make sure that such students don't have to structure their learning and find meaning by themselves. For example, when they go to the library to research, make sure they have a graphic organizer such as a data retrieval chart that they can use to fill in with specific information rather than aimlessly find books and take notes on an unfocused topic.

If the situation gets particularly troublesome, it's time to confer with parents and, as appropriate and with parent permission, students' coaches or religious leaders. We may want to consult the school social worker and psychologist as well as any adult in the building with whom students have formed a positive relationship. Through the conferencing, parents may decide to consult the family doctor and have a physical exam performed to see if there is an attention deficit disorder. If there is a medical problem, the doctor can recommend treatments, including potentially using small dosages of drugs to curb the behavior. While medicating a student is usually not the first choice of responses for parents and doctors, it has helped some students in my classrooms over the years get their lives back.

One of the last resorts, though it can be helpful in some cases, is an extrinsic reward system. We can provide a daily checklist that lists one to five behaviors students must demonstrate to receive a positive notice from the teacher. We focus on redirecting the behaviors that cause us the most concern as we get students back on track. The checklist helps students create positive habits.

Checklist behaviors could include: bring supplies to class, raise hand before speaking, wait to be called on by the teacher, remain in seat for an appropriate amount of time, and stay on task for an appropriate amount of time. For every three days of successful behavior, students receives a reward—other than food. Adolescence and early adolescence are the most common ages for eating disorders to begin, and we don't want to add to any issues that may arise, nor do we want students to think they are only successful and happy when they are eating.

Alfie Kohn (1993) and others would say that in the long run, rewards for positive behavior actually do more damage than good. In general, I agree, which is why in the past twenty-five years I've used the checklist and reward approach with fewer than 5 percent of my students. But in some cases, a checklist and reward system may be the best way to jar students out of their complacency about the impact of their disruptive behavior. It's one possibility to consider, if nothing else helps. We can wean students from the rewards over time.

In some serious situations, I've asked parents to take time from work and sit with their children during my class for a day or more to keep the students on task. It also reinforces that everyone is on the same page and we mean what we say. However, we need to be sensitive when using this approach, because we do not want to cause more dysfunction in the family. It could be very humiliating if parents admonish their children inappropriately in front of classmates. Parents who sit quietly and keep their children focused through eye contact and short, calmly spoken directions are the most effective. Advise them about effective techniques ahead of time. It's surprising how many parents are willing to come to the school for this purpose and how many employers are willing to let parents off work for an hour or so to provide this kind of support for their children.

General Differentiation Strategies Employed

- Make students aware of the problem.

- Create preferential seating.

- Provide structure.

- Make small successes attainable.

- Seek advice from colleagues and other professionals.

- Give clear and frequent feedback.

- Practice new behaviors in short chunks.

- Incorporate students into a lesson's presentation.

- Involve parents.

- Be discreet.

- Provide ways to diffuse the poor behaviors.

- Provide students with choices.

A Few Quick Reminders

It's helpful to spend time building your differentiated toolkit. Try some of the strategies I've suggested, adapt them, and create some of your own. Read, read again, and read some more. There are hundreds of books and professional journals available to you any time you want to access them.

Each time you read them, write your reactions along the top and in the margins and record the great ideas you think will work with your students. Join professional listservs, ask mentors and colleagues for advice, ask your students for advice, watch training videos, attend pertinent conferences every single year of your career, and experiment. Don't be afraid to invent things right on the spot, either. Sometimes the best learning experiences we provide are not reflected in our lesson plans.

A Final Word: Three Tips to Begin the Journey

You've now seen the process for designing differentiated lessons from behind the scenes and in depth. I hope you've discovered some appealing and practical ideas. For additional resources, you may wish to consult the Recommended Resources section. You should be mentally outfitted and ready for the next step, putting some of these ideas into practice.

Let's get started: Do you remember the first step?

Identify your essential understandings, questions, benchmarks, objectives, skills, standards, and/or learner outcomes.

How long should this part take? More than a day? Yes. Need to unpack the standards for yourself? Yes. Need to check your objectives with others? Yes. Now you're rolling—go for it! If you want a one-page review of the planning steps all in one place, check out the Appendix. There are several pages of material you can photocopy and place in your lesson-plan book as reminders for what to do.

As you start writing your differentiated lessons, keep in mind three tips.

1. Start Small

Focus on one element in your teaching unit this week. Use one strategy or approach you've read in the book. Next week or next month, try another. Remember that providing differentiation for all of your students, much less accommodating every student in a single class, every day is impossible. No one can expect you to do this. Our charge is to approximate the goal the best we can while also maintaining healthy habits in our daily lives: seeking a balance between our professional and personal responsibilities. We can't provide much to our students if we feel besieged in all parts of our lives. Once again, remind yourself that you don't have to incorporate all of these ideas at once. Choose one and really explore it for a portion of the year, then build on it.

2. Work with a Colleague

One of the best things you can do for your students is to try these ideas while working with a partner. Your colleague doesn't have to be in the same classroom with you, but pick someone who knows what you're trying to do and can provide timely feedback and support. Once you try the ideas, write or talk about them with other professionals who will respond to your comments.

3. Revisit Those Ten Important Questions

Finally, before you close this book, reflect on your responses to the ten questions I posed in the first chapter, which describe a successfully differentiating teacher's mind-set.

1. Are we willing to teach in whatever way is necessary for students to learn best, even if the approach doesn't match our own preferences?

2. Do we have the courage to do what works, not just what's easiest?

3. Do we actively seek to understand our students' knowledge, skills, and talents so we can provide an appropriate match for their learning needs? And once we discover their individual strengths and weaknesses, do we actually adapt our instruction to respond to their needs?

4. Do we continually build a large and diverse repertoire of instructional strategies so we have more than one way to teach?

5. Do we organize our classrooms for students' learning or for our teaching?

6. Do we keep up-to-date on the latest research about learning, students' developmental growth, and our content specialty areas?

7. Do we ceaselessly self-analyze and reflect on our lessons—including our assessments—searching for ways to improve?

8. Are we open to critique?

9. Do we push students to become their own education advocates and give them the tools to do so?

10. Do we regularly close the gap between knowing what to do and actually doing it?

Your responses to these questions will chart your course for differentiation, and they will serve as an early indicator of your potential for success with differentiated lesson planning and implementation. The strategies and insights described in this book make sense and are worth doing only if we accept the premise and positive attributes of differentiation. If you embrace the principles of differentiation, you'll be in a better position to apply the craft deftly, and even better, you'll be eager to do so. Differentiation is the way to teach smarter, not harder; to feel liberated, not burdened.

Enjoy the journey, and when you get a chance, record your insights for the rest of us to consider. There are many ways to share: magazine articles; blog postings; podcasts; contributions to an email list; conversations at professional conferences, at faculty meetings, or with neighborhood groups. You could become a teacher mentor, start a study group at your school, or write a book. If you're looking for someone to listen to your great ideas and questions, my email address is **rwormeli@cox.net**. If it changes, I'll let my publisher know in case you want to share something. Most of the authors of the resources listed in the Recommended Resources section would also appreciate hearing your wisdom. It takes all of us, contributing and collaborating, to achieve the level of excellence our students deserve.

Recommended Resources

This is by no means a comprehensive list. It represents what one person has experienced as worthwhile resources for teachers' professional development regarding differentiation. I've recommended and used these resources in schools with great success. Only books and resources with practical ideas were included. There are new and helpful materials coming out every year. Be sure to look for them.

Though there are many publishers and professional development companies with excellent speakers and resources on differentiation, the top three in my twenty-seven-year experience are Association for Supervision and Curriculum Development (ASCD): **www.ascd.org**, Staff Development for Educators (SDE): **www.sde.com**, and Corwin Press: **www.corwinpress.com**. Carolyn Coil's company, Pieces of Learning, is also helpful: **www.piecesoflearning.com**. If you want to keep up to date with what's happening in differentiated instruction, get on their mailing lists.

There are many resources included here. Teachers and administrators often ask me, "Which resource would you recommend for those of us just starting to learn how to differentiate instruction?" In response, I've placed an asterisk next to the resources that provide great advice for first-time differentiators. This doesn't mean the same resources wouldn't be helpful to experienced differentiating teachers, or that other sources wouldn't have material useful to beginners.

I have included separate sections for those who may be interested in resources associated with cognitive science, assessment, and grading that can further help us differentiate, as well as sections listing great videos and websites dedicated to differentiation.

Books on Differentiation

Beers, Kylene. 2003. *When Kids Can't Read What Teachers Can Do.* Portsmouth, NH: Heinemann.

Beers, Kylene, & Samuels, Barabara G. 1998. *Into Focus: Understanding and Creating Middle School Readers.* Norwood, MA: Christopher-Gordon.

Bender, William N. 2002. *Differentiating Instruction for Students With Learning Disabilities: Best Teaching Practices for General and Special Educators.* Thousand Oaks, CA: Corwin.

An asterisk indicates a great source for first-time differentiators.

* ———. 2005. *Differentiating Math Instruction: Strategies That Work for K–8 Classrooms!* Thousand Oaks, CA: Corwin.

* Benjamin, Amy. 2002. *Differentiating Instruction: A Guide for Middle and High School Teachers.* Larchmont, NY: Eye on Education.

* Blaz, Deborah. 2006. *Differentiated Instruction: A Guide for Foreign Language Teachers.* Larchmont, NY: Eye on Education.

* Burke, Kay. 2001. *What to Do With the Kid Who …: Developing Cooperation, Self-Discipline, and Responsibility in the Classroom.* Upper Saddle River, NJ: Pearson/Skylight Professional Development.

Burns, Deborah E., Sandra N. Kaplan, Jann H. Leppien, Jeanne H. Purcell, Cindy A. Strickland, and Carol Ann Tomlinson. 2005. *The Parallel Curriculum in the Classroom, Book 1: Essays for Application Across the Content Areas, K–12* and *Book 2: Units for Application Across Content Areas, K–12.* Thousand Oaks, CA: Corwin.

* Chapman, Carolyn, and Gayle H. Gregory, 2001. *Differentiated Instructional Strategies: One Size Doesn't Fit All.* Thousand Oaks, CA: Corwin.

Chapman, Carolyn, and Rita King. 2003. *Differentiated Instructional Strategies for Writing in the Content Areas* and *Differentiated Instructional Strategies for Reading in the Content Areas.* Thousand Oaks, CA: Corwin.

* Coil, Carolyn. 2007. *Successful Teaching in the Differentiated Classroom.* Marion, IL: Pieces of Learning.

Deshler, Donald D. 2005. *Teaching Adolescents with Disabilities: Accessing the General Education Curriculum.* Thousand Oaks, CA: Corwin.

* Dodge, Judith. 2006. *Differentiation in Action: A Complete Resource with Research-Supported Strategies to Help You Plan and Organize*

Differentiated Instruction and Achieve Success with All Learners. New York: Scholastic.

* Drapeau, Patti. 2004. *Differentiated Instruction: Making It Work: A Practical Guide to Planning, Managing, and Implementing Differentiated Instruction to Meet the Needs of All Learners.* New York: Scholastic.

* Fogarty, R. 2001. *Differentiated Learning: Different Strokes for Different Folks.* Chicago: Fogarty and Associates.

* Forsten Char, Gretchen Goodman, Jim Grant, Betty Hollas, and Donna Whyte. 2006. *The More Ways You TEACH, the More Students You REACH: 86 Strategies for Differentiating Instruction.* Peterborough, NH: Crystal Springs Books.

* Forsten, Char, Jim Grant, and Betty Hollas. 2001. *Differentiated Instruction: Different Strategies for Different Learners.* Peterborough, NH: Crystal Springs Books.

* ———. 2003. *Differentiating Textbooks: Strategies to Improve Student Comprehension and Motivation.* Peterborough, NH: Crystal Springs Books.

Frender, Gloria. 2004. *Learning to Learn: Strengthening Study Skills and Brain Power*, rev. ed. Nashville, TN: Incentive Publications.

Gallagher, Kelly. 2004. *Deeper Reading: Comprehending Challenging Texts, 4–12.* Portland, ME: Stenhouse.

Gartin, B. C., N. L. Murdick, M. Imbeau, and D. E. Perner. 2002. *Differentiated Instruction with Students with Developmental Disabilities in the General Education Classroom.* Arlington, VA: Council for Exceptional Children.

Glynn, Carol. 2001. *Learning on their Feet: A Sourcebook for Kinesthetic Learning Across the Curriculum.* Shoreham, VT: Discover Writing Press.

Gregory, Gayle H. 2003. *Differentiated Instructional Strategies in Practice: Training, Implementation, and Supervision.* Thousand Oaks, CA: Corwin.

———. 2005. *Differentiating Instruction with Style: Aligning Teacher and Learner Intelligences for Maximum Achievement.* Thousand Oaks, CA: Corwin.

Gregory, Gayle H., and Lin Kuzmich. 2004. *Data Driven Differentiation in the Standards-Based Classroom.* Thousand Oaks, CA: Corwin.

———. 2004. *Differentiated Literacy Strategies for Student Growth and*

Achievement in Grades K–6. Thousand Oaks, CA: Corwin.

———. 2005. *Differentiated Literacy Strategies for Student Growth and Achievement in Grades 7–12.* Thousand Oaks, CA: Corwin

Harwell, Joan M. 2001. *Complete Learning Disabilities Handbook: Ready-to-Use Strategies and Activities for Teaching Students with Learning Disabilities*, 2nd ed. San Francisco, CA: Jossey-Bass.

* Heacox, Diane. 2000. *Differentiated Instruction in the Regular Classroom, Grades 3–12.* Minneapolis, MN: Free Spirit Publishing.

* Hollas, Betty. 2005. *Differentiating Instruction in a Whole-Group Setting (3–8): Taking the Easy First Steps into Differentiation.* Peterborough, NH: Crystal Springs Books.

———. 2007. *Differentiating Instruction in a Whole-Group Setting (7–12): Taking the Easy First Steps into Differention.* Peterborough, NH: Crystal Springs Books.

Hunter, Alyce, and Barbara King-Shaver. 2003. *Differentiated Instruction in the English Classroom: Content, Process, Product, and Assessment.* Portsmouth, NH: Heinemann.

Karten, Toby J. 2004. *Inclusion Strategies that Work! Aligning Student Strengths with Standards.* Thousand Oaks, CA: Corwin.

Kohn, Alfie 2000. *What to Look for in a Classroom.* San Francisco, CA: Jossey-Bass.

Marzano, Robert J. 1992. *A Different Kind of Classroom: Teaching with Dimensions of Learning.* Alexandria, VA: Association for Supervision and Curriculum Development.

Marzano, Robert J., Debra J. Pickering, and Jane E. Pollock. 2001. *Classroom Instruction That Works: Research-Based Strategies for Increasing Student Achievement.* Alexandria, VA: Association for Supervision and Curriculum Development.

McCarney, Stephen B. 2006. *Pre-Referral Intervention Manual.* Columbia, MO: Hawthorne Educational Services.

McTighe, Jay, and Carol Ann Tomlinson. 2006. *Integrating Differentiated Instruction and Understanding by Design: Connecting Content and Kids.* Alexandria, VA: Association for Supervision and Curriculum Development.

Moll, Anne M., ed. 2003. *Differentiated Instruction Guide for Inclusive Teaching (Grades 3–12).* Port Chester, NY: Dude Publishing.

* Northey, Sheryn Spencer. 2005. *Handbook on Differentiated*

Instruction for Middle and High Schools. Larchmont, NY: Eye on Education.

Novak, John, and William Watson Purkey. 1996. *Inviting School Success: A Self-Concept Approach to Teaching, Learning, and Democratic Practice*. Belmont, CA: Wadsworth.

Renzulli, Joseph S. 2001. *Enriching Curriculum for All Students*. Minneapolis, MN: Skylight Training and Publishing.

* Rogers, Spence, Jim Ludington, and Shari Graham, 1997. *Motivation and Learning: A Teacher's Guide to Building Excitement for Learning and Igniting the Drive for Quality*. Evergreen, CO: Peak Learning Systems.

* Rutherford, Paula. 2002. *Instruction for All Students*. Alexandria, VA: Just ASK Publications.

* Silver, Debbie. 2003. *Drumming to the Beat of a Different Marcher: Finding the Rhythm for Teaching a Differentiated Classroom*. Nashville, TN: Incentive Publications.

* ———. *Differentiated Instruction Planner*. Nashville, TN: Incentive Publications.

Sollman, Carolyn, Barbara Emmons, and Judith Paolini, 1994. *Through the Cracks*. New York: Sterling.

Strong, Richard W., Harvey F. Silver, and Matthew J. Perini. 2001. *Teaching What Matters Most: Standards and Strategies for Raising Student Achievement*. Alexandria, VA: Association for Supervision and Curriculum Development.

Strong, Richard W., Harvey F. Silver, Matthew J. Perini, and Gregory M. Tuculescu. 2002. *Reading for Academic Success: Powerful Strategies for Struggling, Average, and Advanced Readers, Grades 7–12*. Thousand Oaks, CA: Corwin.

* Tilton, Linda. 2003. *The Teacher's Toolbox for Differentiating Instruction: 700 Strategies, Tips, Tools, and Techniques*. Shorewood, MN: Covington Cove Publications.

* Tomlinson, Carol Ann. 1995. *How to Differentiate Instruction in Mixed-Ability Classrooms*, 2nd ed. Alexandria, VA: Association for Supervision and Curriculum Development.

* ———. 1999. *The Differentiated Classroom: Responding to the Needs of All Learners*. Alexandria, VA: Association for Supervision and Curriculum Development.

———. 2003. *Fulfilling the Promise of the Differentiated Classroom:*

Strategies and Tools for Responsive Teaching. Alexandria, VA: Association for Supervision and Curriculum Development.

Tomlinson, Carol Ann, and Caroline C. Eidson 2003. *Differentiation in Practice: A Resource Guide for Differentiating Curriculum, Grades K–5*. Alexandria, VA: Association for Supervision and Curriculum Development.

————. 2003. *Differentiation in Practice: A Resource Guide for Differentiating Curriculum, Grades 5–9*. Alexandria, VA: Association for Supervision and Curriculum Development.

Tomlinson, Carol Ann, and Cindy A. Strickland. 2005. *Differentiation in Practice: A Resource Guide for Differentiating Curriculum, Grades 9–12*. Alexandria, VA: Association for Supervision and Curriculum Development.

Tomlinson, Carol Ann, and Sally M. Reis. 2004. *Differentiation for Gifted and Talented Students*. Thousand Oaks, CA: Corwin.

Tovani, Cris. 2001. *I Read It, But I Don't Get It*. Portland, ME: Stenhouse.

* Winebrenner, Susan, and Pamela Espeland. 1996. *Teaching Kids With Learning Difficulties in the Regular Classroom: Strategies and Techniques Every Teacher Can Use to Challenge and Motivate Struggling Students*. Minneapolis, MN: Free Spirit Publishing.

* ————. 2000. *Teaching Gifted Kids in the Regular Classroom: Strategies and Techniques Every Teacher Can Use to Meet the Academic Needs of the Gifted and Talented*. rev. ed. Minneapolis, MN: Free Spirit Publishing.

Wormeli, Rick. 2001. *Meet Me in the Middle*. Portland, ME: Stenhouse.

————. 2005. *Summarization in Any Subject*. Alexandria, VA: Association for Supervision and Curriculum Development.

Books on Cognitive Science That Help Us Differentiate

Armstrong, Thomas. 1998. *Awakening Genius in the Classroom*. Alexandria, VA: Association for Supervision and Curriculum Development.

* ————. 2000. *Multiple Intelligences in the Classroom*. 2nd ed. Alexandria, VA: Association for Supervision and Curriculum Development.

————. 2003. *The Multiple Intelligences of Reading and Writing: Making the Words Come Alive*. Alexandria, VA: Association for Supervision and Curriculum Development.

* Campbell, Bruce, Linda Campbell, and Dee Dickinson. 2003. *Teaching and Learning Through Multiple Intelligences*, 3rd ed. Boston, MA: Allyn and Bacon.

Goleman, Daniel. 1997. *Emotional Intelligence: Why It Can Matter More Than I.Q.* New York: Bantam.

Hallowell, Edward M., and John J. Ratey. 1994. *Driven to Distraction: Recognizing and Coping with Attention Deficit Disorder from Childhood Through Adulthood*. New York: Pantheon.

Hyerle, David. 2000. *A Field Guide to Visual Tools*. Alexandria, VA: Association for Supervision and Curriculum Development.

* Jensen, Eric. 2000. *Different Brains, Different Learners*. Thousand Oaks, CA: Corwin.

Levine, Mel. 1992. *All Kinds of Minds*. Cambridge, MA: Educators Publishing Service

————. 2003. *The Myth of Laziness*. New York: Simon and Schuster.

Parks, S., and H. Black. 1992. *Organizing Thinking: Book Two*. Pacific Grove, CA: Critical Thinking Press and Software.

Philip, Raleigh T. 2006. *Engaging 'Tweens and Teens: A Brain-Compatible Approach to Reaching Middle and High School Students*. Thousand Oaks, CA: Corwin.

* Sousa, David. 2001. *How the Special Needs Brain Learns*. 3rd ed. Thousand Oaks, CA: Corwin.

* ————. 2002. *How the Gifted Brain Learns*. Thousand Oaks, CA: Corwin.

————. 2004. *How the Brain Learns to Read*. Thousand Oaks, CA: Corwin.

* ————. 2005. *How the Brain Learns*. 3rd ed. Thousand Oaks, CA: Corwin.

* Sprenger, Marilee 2001. *Becoming a "Wiz" at Brain-Based Teaching: How to Make Every Year Your Best Year*. 2nd ed. Thousand Oaks, CA: Corwin.

————. 2003. *Differentiation Through Learning Styles and Memory*. Thousand Oaks, CA: Corwin.

* ———. 2005. *How to Teach So Students Remember*. Alexandria, VA: Association for Supervision and Curriculum Development.

Sternberg, Robert J., and Elena L. Grigorenko. 2001. *Teaching for Successful Intelligence: To Increase Student Learning and Achievement*. Minneapolis, MN: Skylight Training and Publishing.

* Strauch, Barbara. 2004. *The Primal Teen*. New York: Anchor.

Tate, Marcia L. 2003. *Worksheets Don't Grow Dendrites: 20 Instructional Strategies That Engage the Brain*. Thousand Oaks, CA: Corwin.

———. 2005. *Reading and Language Arts Worksheets Don't Grow Dendrites: 20 Literacy Strategies That Engage the Brain*. Thousand Oaks, CA: Corwin.

Wolfe, Patricia. 2001. *Brain Matters: Translating Research into Classroom Practice*. Alexandria, VA: Association for Supervision and Curriculum Development.

Books on Assessment and Grading That Help Us Differentiate

* Brookhart, Susan M. 2004. *Grading*. Upper Saddle River, NJ: Pearson-Merrill, Prentice Hall.

* Coil, Carolyn. 2004. *Standards-Based Activities and Assessments for Differentiated Instruction*. Marion, IL: Pieces of Learning.

Guskey, Thomas R., and Jane Bailey. 2001. *Developing Grading and Reporting Systems for Student Learning*. Thousand Oaks, CA: Corwin.

Marzano, Robert. 2000. *Transforming Classroom Grading*. Alexandria, VA: Association for Supervision and Curriculum Development.

Nolen, Susan Bobbitt, and Catherine S. Taylor. 2005. *Classroom Assessment: Supporting Teaching and Learning in Real Classrooms*. Upper Saddle River, NJ: Pearson–Merrill, Prentice Hall.

* O'Connor, Ken. 2002. *How to Grade for Learning: Linking Grades to Standards*. Thousand Oaks, CA: Corwin.

Popham, W. James. 2004. *Classroom Assessment: What Teachers Need to Know*. 4th ed. Upper Saddle River, NJ: Pearson Education.

Stiggins, Richard J. 2000. *Student-Involved Classroom Assessment*. 3rd ed. Upper Saddle River, NJ: Prentice Hall.

* Stiggins, Richard J., Judith Arter, Jan Chappuis, and Stephen Chappuis. 2004. *Classroom Assessment for Student Learning: Doing It Right—*

Using It Well. Portland, OR: Assessment Training Institute.

* Wormeli, Rick. 2006. *Fair Isn't Always Equal: Assessment and Grading in the Differentiated Classroom*. Portland, ME: Stenhouse.

Videos on Differentiation

* Lavoie, Richard. 1989. *How Difficult Can This Be? The F.A.T. City Workshop*. Washington, D.C.: WETA Video.

* Tomlinson, Carol Ann. 2001. *At Work in the Differentiated Classroom*. Alexandria, VA: Association for Supervision and Curriculum Development [*Tape one of this three-tape series uses my classroom practice to demonstrate planning and instruction ideas*.]

* ———. 2005. *The Common Sense of Differentiation: Meeting Specific Learner Needs in the Regular Classroom*. Alexandria, VA: Association for Supervision and Curriculum Development.

* ———. 2001. *A Visit to a Differentiated Classroom*. Alexandria, VA: Association for Supervision and Curriculum Development.

* ———. 2003. *Instructional Strategies for the Differentiated Classroom, Tapes 1–7*. Alexandria, VA: Association for Supervision and Curriculum Development.

Websites Dedicated to Differentiated Practices

www.help4teachers.com

www.middleweb.com

http://members.shaw.ca/priscillatheroux/

www.kidsource.com/kidsource/content/diff_instruction.html

www.sde.com

www.learnerslink.com

www.ldonline.org

www.ascd.org/portal/site/ascd/menuitem.3adeebc6736780dddeb3ffdb621
     08a0c/

www.montgomeryschoolsmd.org/curriculum/enriched

www.NAGC.org

The pages in this appendix can be photocopied and used with students or can be inserted in your lesson-plan book for quick reference.

Mind-Set of Successfully Differentiating Teachers

1. Are we willing to teach in whatever way is necessary for students to learn best, even if the approach doesn't match our own preferences?

2. Do we have the courage to do what works, not just what's easiest?

3. Do we actively seek to understand our students' knowledge, skills, and talents so we can provide an appropriate match for their learning needs? And once we discover their individual strengths and weaknesses, do we actually adapt our instruction to respond to their needs?

4. Do we continually build a large and diverse repertoire of instructional strategies so we have more than one way to teach?

5. Do we organize our classrooms for students' learning or for our teaching?

6. Do we keep up to date on the latest research about learning, students' developmental growth, and our content specialty areas?

7. Do we ceaselessly self-analyze and reflect on our lessons—including our assessments—searching for ways to improve?

8. Are we open to critique?

9. Do we push students to become their own education advocates and give them the tools to do so?

10. Do we regularly close the gap between knowing what to do and actually doing it?

Two Charges of Differentiation

1. Do whatever it takes to maximize students' learning instead of relying on one-size-fits-all, whole-class methods of instruction.

2. Prepare students to handle anything in their current and future lives that is not differentiated, i.e., to become their own learning advocates.

Frame of Reference: Great teachers do what is fair (developmentally appropriate), and what is fair isn't always equal.

Differentiated Lesson-Planning Sequence

Steps to Take Before *Designing the Learning Experiences*

1. Identify your essential understandings, questions, benchmarks, objectives, skills, standards, and/or learner outcomes.

2. Identify those students who have special needs, and start thinking about how you will adapt your instruction to ensure they can learn and achieve.

3. Design formative and summative assessments.

4. Design and deliver preassessments based on summative assessments and identified objectives.

5. Adjust assessments and objectives based on further thinking while designing the assessments.

Steps to Take While *Designing and Implementing the Learning Experiences*

1. Design the learning experiences for students based on the information gathered from those preassessments; your knowledge of your students; and your expertise with the curriculum, cognitive theory, and students at this stage of human development.

2. Run a mental tape of each step in the lesson sequence to make sure that the process makes sense for your diverse group of students and will help the lesson will run smoothly.

3. Review your plans with a colleague.

4. Obtain/create materials needed for the lesson.

5. Conduct the lesson.

6. Adjust formative and summative assessments and objectives as necessary based on observations and data collected while teaching the lessons.

Steps to Take After *Providing the Learning Experiences*

1. With students, evaluate the lesson's success. What evidence do you have that students grasped the important concepts and skills? What worked and what didn't, and why?

2. Record advice about possible changes to make when you repeat this lesson in future years.

Helpful Differentiation and Cognition Approaches

For Differentiation

- Tiering
- Respectful Tasks
- Compacting the Curriculum
- The Football and the Anchor: Teaching a Variety of Levels at the Same Time
- Flexible Grouping
- Teacher-Student Collaboration
- Exit Cards
- Clock or Appointment Partners
- Personal Agendas
- Different, Not More or Less
- Assess and Adjust
- Modify Options: Content, Process, Product, Affect, Learning Environment
- Models of Instruction
- Scaffold Instruction

For Cognition

- Building Background Knowledge
- Priming the Brain and Structuring Information
- Primacy-Recency Effect
- Examples and Nonexamples
- Hydration
- Emotional Content
- Movement
- Novelty
- Meeting Survival Needs
- Memory Ideas
- Social Interaction

Planning for the Three Types of Assessments

Summative Assessment Ideas:

Formative Assessment Ideas:
[Note the ample space to emphasize formative over summative.]

Preassessment Ideas:

Essential and Enduring Knowledge (EEK) and Know, Understand, and Do (KUD)

Curriculum that is essential and enduring that all students must learn:

Curriculum that is nice to know if we have the time and need for it (enrichment material):

Objectives/Outcomes students should *know*:

Objectives/Outcomes students should *understand*:

Objectives/Outcomes students should *do*:

Clock Partners

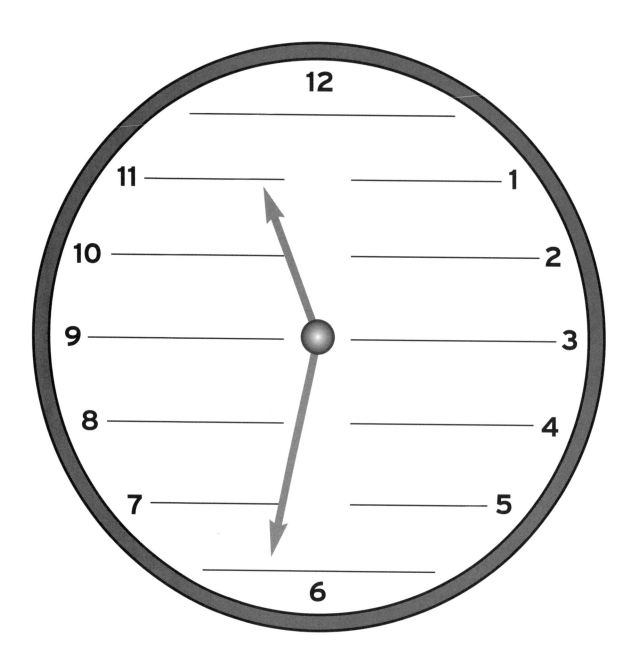

The Football Sequence

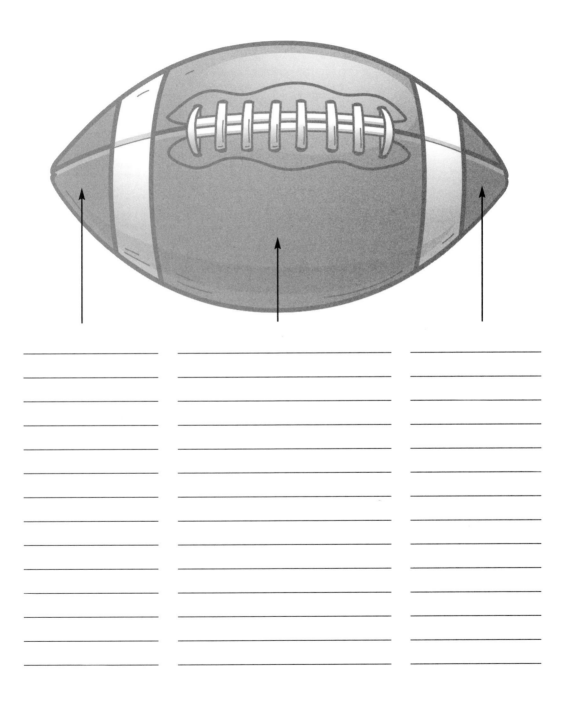

The Anchor Lesson Design

Components of a Great Lesson

1. Inviting Thinking Activities

2. A Set Context and Objectives

3. Outlined Agenda/Itinerary

4. Learning Experiences

5. Sponges (short, yet substantive activities related to the day's learning)

6. Formative and Summative Assessments

7. Summarization/Closure Tasks

8. Advanced Look at the Next Lesson

In all units of instruction, there should be time for whole-class, small-group, and individual experiences with content and skills.

Ebb and Flow of Experiences

Back and forth over course of unit

Individual Small Group Whole Group Small Group Individual

Source: Based on Carol Ann Tomlinson's *Ebb and Flow of Experiences from How to Differentiate in Mixed-Ability Classrooms, 2nd ed.* Adapted by permission of the publisher, Association for Supervision and Curriculum Development.

References

Bloom, Benjamin S., and David R. Krathwohl. 1956. *Taxonomy of Educational Objectifes: Handbook 1: Cognitive Domain*. New York: Longman.

Canady, Robert Lynn, and Michael Rettig. 1996. *Teaching in the Block: Strategies for Engaging Active Learners*. Larchmont, NY: Eye on Education.

Costa, Art, and Bena Kallick. 2000. *Habits of Mind* series. Alexandria, VA: Association for Supervision and Curriculum Development.

Culham, Ruth. 2003. *6+1 Traits of Writing: The Complete Guide*. New York: Scholastic.

Dunn, Rita. 2007. Learning Styles. International Learning Styles Network. www.learningstyles.net.

Frank, Anne. 1993. *The Diary of a Young Girl*. Translated by B.M. Mooyaart. New York: Bantam.

Gallagher, Kelly. 2004. *Deeper Reading: Comprehending Challenging Texts, 4–12*. Portland, ME: Stenhouse.

Gardner, Howard. 1983. *Frames of Mind: The Theory of Multiple Intelligences*. New York: Basic Books.

Gregorc, Anthony. 1999–2007. Gregorc Associates, Inc. www.gregorc.com

Hollas, Betty. 2005. *Differentiating Instruction in a Whole-Group Setting (3–8): Taking the Easy First Steps into Differentiation*. Peterborough, NH: Crystal Springs Books.

———. 2007. *Differentiating Instruction in a Whole-Group Setting (7–12): Taking the Easy First Steps into Differention.* Peterborough, NH: Crystal Springs Books.

Hunter, Madeline. 1993. *Enhancing Teaching.* New York: MacMillan.

Hunter, Robin. 1994. *Madeline Hunter's Mastery Teaching: Increasing Instructional Effectiveness in Elementary and Secondary Schools.* Thousand Oaks, CA: Corwin.

Jensen, Eric. 2000. *Different Brains, Different Learners.* Thousand Oaks, CA: Corwin Press.

———. 2005. *Teaching with the Brain in Mind.* Alexandria, VA: Association for Supervision and Curriculum Development.

———. 2006. *Enriching the Brain: How to Maximize Every Learner's Potential.* San Francisco: Jossey-Bass.

Kohn, Alfie. 1993. *Punished by Rewards: The Trouble with Gold Stars, Incentive Plans, A's, Praise, and Other Bribes.* New York: Houghton Mifflin.

Lounsbury, John H. 2006. "These 'Things' I Believe." William Alexander Memorial Lecture at the National Middle School Association Annual Conference, Nashville, TN.

Macaulay, David. 1979. *Motel of the Mysteries.* New York: Scholastic.

Magorian, Michelle. 1982. *Good Night, Mr. Tom.* New York: Harper & Row.

Marzano, Robert J. 1992. *A Different Kind of Classroom: Teaching with Dimensions of Learning.* Alexandria, VA: Association for Supervision and Curriculum Development.

Marzano, Robert J. 2004. *Building Background Knowledge for Academic Achievement.* Alexandria, VA: Association for Supervision and Curriculum Development.

Marzano, Robert J., Debra J. Pickering, and Jane E. Pollock. 2001. *Classroom Instruction That Works: Research-Based Strategies for Increasing Student Achievement.* Alexandria, VA: Association for Supervision and Curriculum Development.

Matas, Carol. 1989. *Lisa's War.* New York: Atheneum.

McCarthy, Bernice. 2007. About Learning. www.aboutlearning.com.

McTighe, Jay, and Grant Wiggins. 2004. *The Understanding by Design Professional Development Workbook.* Alexandria, VA: Association for Supervision and Curriculum Development.

Myers and Briggs Foundation. 2007. The Myers and Briggs Foundation. www.myersbriggs.org.

Robertson, William C. 2002. *Stop Faking It! Force and Motion*. Arlington, VA: National Science Teachers Association.

Sheffield, Charles. 1996. *Georgia on My Mind and Other Places*. New York: Tor Books.

Sousa, David. 2006. *How the Brain Learns*. 3rd ed. Thousand Oaks, CA: Corwin Press.

Spandel, Vicki. 2004. *Creating Writers Through 6-Trait Writing Assessment and Instruction*. 4th ed. Boston, MA: Allyn and Bacon.

Sprenger, Marilee. 2005. *How to Teach So Students Remember*. Alexandria, VA: Association for Supervision and Curriculum Development.

Strauch, Barbara. 2004. *The Primal Teen*. New York: Anchor.

Sylwester, Robert. 2007. *The Adolescent Brain: Reaching for Autonomy*. Thousand Oaks, CA: Corwin Press.

Tomlinson, Carol Ann. 1999. *The Differentiated Classroom: Responding to the Needs of All Learners*. Alexandria, VA: Association for Supervision and Curriculum Development.

Tomlinson, Carol Ann. 2001a. *At Work in the Differentiated Classroom*. Video series. Alexandria, VA: Association for Supervision and Curriculum Development.

Tomlinson, Carol Ann. 2001b. *How to Differentiate Instruction in Mixed-Ability Classrooms*, 2nd ed. Alexandria, VA: Association for Supervision and Curriculum Development.

Tomlinson, Carol Ann, and Cindy Strickland. 2005. *Differentiation in Practice: A Resource Guide for Differentiating Curriculum, Grades 9–12*. Alexandria, VA: Association for Supervision and Curriculum Development.

Tovani, Cris. 2001. *I Read It, But I Don't Get It*. Portland, ME: Stenhouse.

Wiggins, Grant, and Jay McTighe. 2005. *Understanding by Design*. 2nd ed. Alexandria, VA: Association for Supervision and Curriculum Development.

Williams, Frank E. 1972. *A Total Creativity Program for Individualizing and Humanizing the Learning Process*. Englewood Cliffs, NJ: Education Technology Publications.

Wolfe, Patricia. 2001. *Brain Matters: Translating Research into Classroom Practice*. Alexandria, VA: Association for Supervision and Curriculum Development.

Wormeli, Rick. 2006. *Fair Isn't Always Equal: Assessing and Grading in the Differentiated Classroom*. Portland, ME: Stenhouse.

Yolen, Jane. 1988. *The Devil's Arithmetic*. New York: Viking Penguin.

Index

4MAT system, 74
Full-spectrum lighting, 107–108

G

Gardner, Howard, 25, 74, 134
Giftedness
    before designing learning experiences and, 18f, 24–26
    differentiated instruction and, 11
    learning experience design and, 16
    responding to student needs and, 48–52
    strategy development and, 39–40
Global economy, need for differentiated instruction and, 3
Goals
    before designing learning experiences and, 22–23
    examples of, 45, 122, 123
Good Night, Mr. Tom, 92
Gradations of mastery. *See* Mastery
Grade-level standards. *See* Standards
Grading
    Fair Isn't Always Equal: Assessment and Grading in the Differentiated Classroom, 86
    resources for, 150
Graduate Assistants, 96f
Graphic organizer, examples of, 47f, 119
Gregorc, Anthony, 74
Grouping
    anchor structure and, 93–97
    components of great lesson and, 163f
    differentiation and, 156
    examples of, 117
    flexible, 75–79
    football structure and, 91–93
    novelty and, 107
    social interaction and, 110–113

H

Habits of Mind, 29
Habits of mind, dimensions of

learning model and, 73
Half class groups. *See* Grouping
Headaches, hydration and, 105
History
    anchor lessons and, 96
    assessment and, 26–31
    background knowledge and, 100
    Cortéz lesson plan and, 26–27, 34–35, 39, 42–46, 46–49, 47f, 53–58
    curriculum and, 19
    drama and, 107–108
    essential understandings and, 23
    football structure and, 92
    learning disabilities and, 1
    lesson planning and, 17, 22–24, 48
    mastery and, 84
    memory and, 110
    narrative authenticity and, 93
    respectful tasks and, 89
    social interaction and, 112
    structure and, 101
Hollas, Betty, 111
Homework
    assessment and, 37
    checking, 103
    direct instruction model and, 73
    examples of, 46
Hook, direct instruction model and, 73
How the Brain Learns, 99, 102
How to Teach So Students Remember, 99, 102
Human development, learning experience design and, 16, 18f, 20
Hunter, Madeline, 72
Hydration, 104–105, 156

I

I Read It, but I Don't Get It, 102
IB classes. *See* International Baccalaureate classes
IEPs. *See* Individual Education Plans
Implementation, of learning experiences. *See* Learning experiences
Incremental learning, examples of, 122

Independent work, 87
    gifted students and, 50
Individual Education Plans, 25, 40
Individual study. *See* Grouping
Inference, 83
Informal differentiation, 61
Information
    differentiated lesson-planning sequence and, 155
    football structure for presentation of, 91–93, 91f
    manipulation of, 86
Input, direct instruction model and, 73
Instruction models, 72–75
Integration, subject/skill, 86
Intellectual considerations, 3. *See also* Giftedness; Learning disabilities
Interests, tiering and, 81
International Baccalaureate classes, 52–53
Intrinsic motivation, 136–137
Irritability, 104–105

J

Jensen, Eric, 99
Journals, before designing learning experiences and, 21

K

Kallick, Bena, 29
Knowledge
    applications of, 127
    background, 100, 106
    before designing learning experiences and, 16
    cognition and, 156
    dimensions of learning model and, 73
    essential and enduring (EEK), 158–159
    examples of, 45
    one-third model and, 73

L

Labeling, 50
Language arts
    anchor lessons and, 97
    editing text scenario and,

teachers and, 106, 156
Styles, learning. *See* Learning
  styles
Subject-specific material, applications of differentiated instruction
  and, 12–13
Summarizing
  direct instruction model and,
    73
  football structure and, 91–93,
    91*f*
  student, 58
Summative assessment
  before designing learning expe-
    riences and, 18*f*, 26–27
  design and implementation of
    learning experiences and, 32,
    59, 61
  differentiated lesson-planning
    sequence and, 155
  formative assessments and, 69
  learning experience design and,
    16, 17
  planning for, 157
Sums of interior angles, sample
  scenario of differentiation and,
  117–119, 118*f*
Sunlight, 107–108
Survival needs, 108–109, 156
Sylwester, Robert, 99
Synthesis of information, 73, 88

T

Talking, 106
Tasks
  differentiation and, 156
  examples of, 123
  respectful, 89–90
Taxonomy
  Bloom's Taxonomy, 86, 111
  sample scenario of differentia-
    tion and, 132–134
  Williams's Taxonomy, 86
Teachers
  availability of, 95
  as colleagues. *See* Colleagues
  feelings of being overwhelmed
    and, 4
  gifted students and, 51–52
  mind-set of those successfully
    differentiating, 154
  relationships with students and,

106, 156
willingness to provide differentiated instruction and, 8–9,
  140–141
Teams. *See* Grouping
Technoids, 96*f*
Tests, before designing learning
  experiences and, 21
Textbooks, before designing learning experiences and, 22
Think-alouds, 129, 130
Tickler files, 63
Tiering
  compacting curriculum and, 90
  defining, 81
  differentiation and, 156
  examples of, 119
  football/anchor metaphors and,
    91–97
  gradations of mastery and,
    83–89
  respectful tasks and, 89–90
  scaffolding instruction and,
    97–98
  Tomlinson's Equalizer and,
    81–83
Time considerations
  assessment and, 69–70
  before designing learning expe-
    riences and, 17–18
  strategy development and, 37
  task completion and, 58
Tomlinson, Carol Ann, 70–71,
  81–83, 85
Tovani, Cris, 102
Triads. *See* Grouping

U

Understandings
  before designing learning expe-
    riences and, 17–24, 18*f*
  concept attainment model and,
    73–74
  design and implementation of
    learning experiences and, 61
  differentiated lesson-planning
    sequence and, 155
  direct instruction model and,
    73
  learning experience design and,
    16

V

Variables, 86
Visual techniques, examples of,
  117, 125, 130

W

Warm-up activities, 103
Web resources, 151
Whole-class groups. *See* Grouping
Wiggins, Grant, 85
Williams's Taxonomy, 86
Winebrenner, Susan, 85
Wolfe, Patricia, 99, 110
Work load, differentiation and,
  65–67
World view, 127
Written techniques, examples of,
  117